The Irish Châte

The Irish Châteaux

In Search of Descendants
of the Wild Geese

Renagh Holohan

&

Jeremy Williams

THE LILLIPUT PRESS

First published 1989 (0 946640 41 6)

New impression 1999 by

THE LILLIPUT PRESS LTD
62-63 Sitric Road, Arbour Hill, Dublin 7, Ireland.

British Library Cataloguing in Publishing Data
Holohan, Renagh, 1947
The Irish Châteaux: in search of descendants of the wild geese

1. Ireland. Castles. History
I. Title
941.5

ISBN 1 901866 34 3

NOTE TO 1999 PRINTING
This new impression of *The Irish Châteaux* contains a
supplementary list of châteaux with Wild Geese connections and
an extended bibliography. Since the book was first published in
1989, three hundred Tiernys foregathered in Arras in 1991 to
celebrate the arrival as a member of the Clare Brigade of their
ancestor Patrick Tierny of Clones three hundred years earlier.
Inevitably, interest in Ireland, then focused on the Limerick
tercentenary of 1991, switched to the bicentenary of the uprising of
1798, further stressing the close relationship between Ireland and
France. A new wine museum in Kinsale maintains contact with the
Irish wines of Bordeaux, while the MacMahon wine of the Duke of
Magenta has been served to the French presidents during
state dinners in Dublin Castle.

Media Conversion by Diskon Technical Services Ltd.,
and set in 11 on 13pt Garamond.
Printed in Dublin by the Elo Press Ltd.

CONTENTS

ILLUSTRATIONS

INTRODUCTION

T HE IRISH, it seems, have always emigrated. Some of these movements are well remembered, some still continue, and some are quite forgotten. However, the emigrants who went to continental Europe in the seventeenth and eighteenth centuries, the Wild Geese, were special. Certainly the myths that have developed about them have no parallel; the celebration of their nobility and their sacrifices, their love of Ireland and of Catholicism is remarkable in itself, but has quite disguised the historical realities of the diaspora.

Poems have been written and songs sung of their sorrowful departures and their feats of daring on the battlefields of Europe. The term Wild Geese to describe these emigrants was used colloquially as far back as Swift's time in the second quarter of the eighteenth century, but the romantic notion of the Wild Geese was only fully developed in the early nineteenth century by Catholic apologists and built up later by Young Irelanders and others concerned with the reconstruction of Irish history in a nationalist paradigm.

The *Oxford English Dictionary* says a wild goose refers to a flighty or foolish person and that it was the nickname given to Irish Jacobites who went over to the Continent on the abdication of James II and later. As early as 1843 M. J. Barry was writing,*

> *The wild geese, the wild geese, 'tis long since they flew,*
> *O'er the billowy ocean's bright bosom of blue.*

The romantic explanation is that the term described recruits for the Irish Brigades on a ship's manifest as it returned to France from the south and south-west coasts of Ireland after unloading its cargo of wine and brandy.

Spirit of the Nation, (Dublin 1845).

Mercenary service was neither unique to Ireland nor were those who partook in it socially homogenous. The phenomenon of young men from the peripheral areas of Europe leaving backward agrarian societies to join the great armies of the Continent was not uncommon during the pre-industrial period. Switzerland, Sweden and Scotland all experienced similar migrations of mercenaries. Sons from every social class were drawn into it.

In Ireland the sons of wealthier Catholic parents left because political and military defeat had led to the confiscation of ancestral lands and because their Catholic religion closed the doors to formal education and to genteel careers in the higher professions, politics or the army. Catholics under the penal laws could not enlist in the British army despite the fact that roughly half of the regular army in the eighteenth century was actually stationed in Ireland and paid for by Irish taxes. Protestants made up some of the numbers but generally in a commercial capacity, as part of a mercantile migration common to maritime trading regions in Western Europe.

The migration of the Wild Geese, running at high if greatly fluctuating levels between the Treaty of Limerick in 1691 and the Peace of Aix-la-Chapelle in 1748, was unusual in its scale and duration. The huge nineteenth-century migrations from Ireland, mostly to the United States of America, have tended to eclipse other earlier movements, but in Irish popular tradition the French migration has a special place – however artificial.

It was highly disparate in character. Some were similar to today's young emigrants, being comparatively well-educated and equipped with marketable skills, and they left because of frustrated personal expectations. A few were committed Jacobites hoping to return to liberate their country, but the great majority were divided between those of a high social status seeking personal advancement in Church, trade or army, and the larger group who were poor, ill-educated, of small-farmer background and without family connections abroad, who went into mercenary service to earn a living. The total number has never been accurately measured, but if the provisional estimate of 50,000 is accepted, the continental migration was a large-scale movement by eighteenth-century standards and stands comparison with the contemporary emigrations from Ulster to colonial America.

The great majority who emigrated never returned. The foot-soldiers who went out in waves from Munster, Connacht and Ulster (rather than from Leinster) have left almost no historical trace outside the military archives. J. G. Simms has written* that there are no records of the descendants of the Irish rank and file, thousands of whom fought for France and for the Stuarts. Scholars presume that they were simply assimilated into the native population and somehow managed to lose their names. Thousands of others died young, either on the battlefield or in outbreaks of camp fever which frequently cut through armies of the day.

The smaller group perpetuated and recorded family traditions and preserved a consciousness of their lineage. Six or eight generations later they are easy to find, and many have meticulous genealogies, drawn up around the turn of the present century when their original pedigrees, admitting them to the French court, were reproduced at a time of increased interest in genealogy.

This richer, educated section also included the clergy who, presumably, have left no direct descendants, and the traders. Some of the clerics returned to Ireland when their education at the Irish Colleges of Paris, Bordeaux, Nantes or Rouen was complete, but until the later eighteenth century, very large numbers were absorbed into French

---

*'The Irish on the Continent, 1691-1800' in T. W. Moody and W. E. Vaughan, *A New History of Ireland*, iv (Oxford 1986).

dioceses, and never returned to the more precarious life at home. The commercial migration, Catholic and Protestant, was at its strongest between the mid-seventeenth and mid-eighteenth centuries, a time of great volatility in the merchant communities of the Irish ports, and of rapidly expanding long-distant Atlantic trade. Some of the Irish merchant emigrés were simply completing their commercial education abroad with one of their father's correspondents, but continental ports, from Ostend and Rouen in the north to Cadiz and Malaga in the south, had significant Irish merchant communities or 'factories' by 1750, composed of first- and second-generation emigrés who could exploit their singular mix of political, linguistic and religious connections to their family's profit.

These complexities were lost sight of in later tradition. The Wild Geese emigration was regarded from nineteenth-century retrospect as a great flow of fighting men leaving Ireland for purely political reasons and making, by their actions, a statement about their aversion to the English in Ireland. Even now, the Wild Geese are often wrongly perceived as that small band of about 100 men, women and children who left with the great northern chieftains, Hugh O'Neill and Ruairí O'Donnell, from Lough Swilly in Donegal in 1607, some years after the Irish defeat at Kinsale. This 'Flight of the Earls' is usually taken to mark the end of Gaelic Catholic Ulster and to have opened the way for the huge Anglo-Scottish plantation.

There were larger emigrations following the Cromwellian victory in 1649-51, when the 1641 rebellion was finally extinguished. But the biggest single wave took place after the Boyne and Limerick. With Louis xvi's enormous land army of France these migrants quickly built up a great reputation for military bravery, and the officers won promotion and status. They married into other Irish families already in France and into the French gentry and nobility.

Numbers were knighted for services to the exiled Stuarts and to the Bourbons, and a record or declaration of anti-English activity at home in Ireland was consequently an advantage in seeking such advancement. The title 'comte' was bestowed by the French kings on individuals admitted to court who showed that their family was of ancient or noble origin. As a courtesy title it carried no rights, but it had some official status and, since it was the family that had been honoured, the title could readily be carried by a relative after the death of the recipient.

The families we have traced in *The Irish Châteaux* are descended from these sons and daughters of Irish gentry. They are now French in all but name, but they retain a strong interest in their background. Genealogies, family trees and histories are on hand to tell their 'romantic' story. Strangely they are almost as out of step with modern France as they are with modern Ireland. *Ancien régime* in attitude, they are almost to a man solidly royalist and universally refer to the Old Pretender, their ancestors' Stuart leader and benefactor, as Jacques Trois and in many cases have called their sons Charles Edouard after Bonny Prince Charlie. Their view of Ireland is decidedly anachronistic: wholly Catholic, 'Celtic' and, in a historical dimension, anti-English.

'*Les Oies Sauvages*' is a term well known and respected in France and, given the current fashion for all things Irish, it is no disadvantage to be able to prove descent from them. Links between the two countries have always been strong. There was the common bond of religion and of opposition to England, and in the seventeenth and eighteenth centuries there was a flourishing exchange of salt, wine, cognac and silk for fish, butter, beef, wool, linen and leather as well as recruits for the Irish Brigades and clerical students.

The close links, weakened by the collapse of the Stuart cause after the 1740s, were severed at the outbreak of the

French Revolution in 1789 when the more conservative elements in Ireland could neither countenance nor understand the anti-Catholic stance taken by so many of its leaders and the subsequent closure of the Irish Colleges, together with the harassment and murder of priests and clerical students.

In 1791 the Irish Brigades were disbanded as a separate unit in the French army; for more than a decade there had been extensive recruitment of all classes and creeds of Irishmen into the British army and navy, and it was quite appropriate for a section of the Irish Brigade officers to form a new regiment in George III's army. Meanwhile, in 1795, Maynooth, outside Dublin, was established as an official, government-funded Catholic seminary. Britain now controlled international trade; it had a stronger economy than France, and it was master of the seas and an expanding empire. Irish contact with France declined dramatically.

The Wild Geese, however, were not forgotten and formed the subject of patriotic poems such as Emily Lawless's 'After Aughrim':*

> She said, 'They gave me of their best,
> They lived, they gave their lives for me;
> I tossed them to the howling waste,
> And flung them to the foaming sea.'
>
> She said, 'I never gave them aught,
> Not mine the power, if mine the will;
> I let them starve, I let them bleed, –
> They bled and starved, and loved me still.'

---

*The poem, cast as an *aisling* and published in 1902, refers to the battle of Aughrim of July 1691, where the French General St Ruth and the Irish leader Patrick Sarsfield were defeated by King William's forces under the Dutch General Ginkle. This opened the way for the Treaty of Limerick the following October.

Introduction

She said, 'Ten times they fought for me,
Ten times they strove with might and main,
Ten times I saw them beaten down,
Ten times they rose, and fought again.'

She said, 'I stayed alone at home,
A dreary woman, grey and cold;
I never asked them how they fared,
Yet still they love me as of old.'

She said, 'I never called them sons,
I almost ceased to breathe their name,
Then caught it echoing down the wind,
Blown backwards from the lips of Fame.'

She said, 'Not mine, not mine that fame;
Far over sea, far over land,
Cast forth like rubbish from my shores,
They won it yonder, sword in hand.'

She said, 'God knows they owe me naught,
I tossed them to the foaming sea,
I tossed them to the howling waste,
Yet still their love comes home to me.'

1: Bignon-Mirabeau

ONE

NORTHERN FRANCE

O'Connors, de la Tour du Pins, O'Mahonys

C'était un château de vallée
L'herbe dressée de trois prairies,
Les bois de pentes, aux chemins
Indéfinis qui s'en allaient,
Les Morailles, les Picardies
Avec leurs châteaux de sapins.

So WROTE the French poet, Patrice de la Tour du Pin of the Château du Bignon-Mirabeau, which his great-great-grandfather, the United Irishman and French general Arthur O'Connor, bought in 1808 when he married an heiress, Eliza de Condorcet, daughter of the philosopher and mathematician. Today the château is the home of the poet's widow, la Comtesse de la Tour du Pin, and, occasionally, of his four daughters. Situated in the village of Le Bignon-Mirabeau, it was once the home of the Marquis de Mirabeau and his revolutionary writer son, Comte de Mirabeau. It is 100 kilometres south of Paris near the town of Nemours and is open to the public during the summer.

Arthur O'Connor was born near Bandon, Co. Cork, in

I BIGNON-MIRABEAU *Built c. 1880 by Ernest Sanson, the favourite architect of Marcel Proust. He specialized in preserving the fittings from châteaux he replaced to give what his clients believed to be the best of both worlds. The library re-uses the chimney-piece dominated by a full-size portrait of General O'Connor; the salon retains the Beauvais tapestries and opens into a turret decorated by the poet de la Tour du Pin, with cut-outs of monkeys, as a distraction from the last war.*

1763, the younger son of Roger Conner, a rich Protestant landowner, possibly of English extraction, and Anne Longfield, sister of Lord Longueville. He first studied law and from 1791 to 1796, when he joined the United Irishmen, was a member of the Irish House of Commons which sat in College Green, Dublin. He was also High Sheriff of Cork during 1791. Initially conservative, during his time as an MP he visited France, met Lafayette, and was so impressed by revolutionary ideas that he became strongly republican and spoke out in favour of Grattan's bill for Catholic Emancipation. His speech, which Wolfe Tone described to General Hoche as "the ablest and honestest speech ever made in the Irish parliament", cost him his seat but secured his fame.

O'Connor travelled to France in 1796 and with his friend Lord Edward Fitzgerald approached the French Directory (also at that time being courted by Tone for the same purpose) to send an expeditionary force to Ireland. O'Connor painted an optimistic picture: Ireland, he argued, was ripe for rebellion and an invasion would quickly take England out of the war with France.

> We only want your help in the first moment. In two months we should have 100,000 men under arms; we ask your assistance only because we know it is your own clear interest to give it, and only on condition that you leave us absolute masters to frame our government as we please.

General Hoche's expedition of 43 ships and 15,000 soldiers sailed from Brest with Tone aboard at Christmas 1796. After a number of initial setbacks it entered Bantry Bay but returned to France when snow and storms, and the absence of any spontaneous rising on the land, forced a retreat.

O'Connor then left France for Ireland where he was on the executive of the Leinster Directory of the United Irishmen with Fitzgerald, Thomas Emmet (brother of Robert), Oliver Bond, a wool merchant, and Dr William

MacNeven. He was arrested in February 1797 following a seditious address published in the *Northern Star* and spent six months in Dublin Castle. He was released untried but, with other leaders of the Leinster Directory, was re-arrested on the crushing of the 1798 rebellion and imprisoned again, first at Kilmainham and then at Fort George in Scotland.

On his release from Fort George after the Peace of Amiens in 1802, O'Connor returned to Paris. An Irish lady, Mrs St George, later Mrs Chenevix Trench, wrote in her diary in Calais that July:

> My eyes presented me with Arthur O'Connor and a group of his associates. His features are regular and his person good. At the moment I saw him he had a dark and scowling but sensible expression. He wore a green handkerchief as a neck cloth and a tri-coloured cockade.

In Paris O'Connor was regarded by Napoleon as the accredited representative of the United Irishmen, and in 1804 he was appointed general of division in the French army. Thomas Emmet's suggestion for an Irish Legion to liberate Ireland was accepted by the emperor, and at his coronation he presented it with a colour which had his own name on one side and a harp, without a crown, and the inscription L'Indépendance d'Irlande, on the other. The uniforms were green.

O'Connor was designated commander of the expedition to Ireland but it never materialized and the Legion saw service instead in Prussia and Spain. It was disbanded in 1815 and although many officers of Irish descent continued to serve in the French army, there was no specific Irish unit and the supply of new recruits fell. Just as the endowment of Maynooth College in 1795 saw a huge decline in students coming to the great Irish Colleges of the Continent for their education, so the relaxation of the penal laws in the second half of the eighteenth century also reduced the need for the sons of the gentry to seek their fortunes in Europe.

The chef de bataillon of the short-lived Irish Legion was the Ennis, Co. Clare-born James Bartholomew Blackwell. In 1776, aged eleven, he enrolled as a student at the Irish College in Paris but, abandoning his medical studies, he joined the army and before the Revolution had become an intimate friend of Danton and Camille Desmoulins. He was prominent at the storming of the Bastille and in 1796 accompanied Wolfe Tone to Bantry Bay and, two years later, Napper Tandy to the Donegal coast.

On their return journey both Blackwell and Tandy, a general in the French army, were arrested at Hamburg and extradited to England. Released after two years Blackwell returned to France and fought under the emperor in the Prussian and Austrian campaigns, dying in Paris in 1820.

After the abortive attempt to send the Legion to Ireland, O'Connor retired from the army. When Napoleon returned from Elba in 1815 the general offered the former emperor his services. The offer was strongly condemned by his fellow French-born Irishman, Henry Clarke, Duc de Feltre, Napoleon's private secretary from 1807 to 1814 and general in his army. Clarke, of whom Wolfe Tone initially thought very little, was a great survivor and later re-aligned himself with the Bourbons, becoming Louis XVIII's minister of war.

The Clarkes, who were originally from Kilkenny, had a long association with the Irish Brigades and the Duc de Feltre's maternal grandfather, William Shee of Limerick, was also an officer in the regiment. The duke's home in Paris was the Hôtel d'Estrées, 79 rue de Grenelle. In Nantes a street is named after him and his portrait hangs in the Musée des Beaux-Arts. The title died out with Clarke's son but was restored by Napoleon III in favour of his great-great-grandson, Charles de Goyon.

In 1807 O'Connor had married Eliza, only daughter of the Marquis de Condorcet, who in 1792 had been president of the National Assembly. Being a Girondist and thus against sending Louis XVI to the guillotine, Condorcet was forced into hiding. He was discovered during the Terror of 1794, jailed and found dead in prison the next day.

In 1808 O'Connor bought the Château de Bignon-Mirabeau, partly with money given to him by Napoleon (according to the Comtesse de la Tour du Pin), and partly with his wife's fortune. In 1834, having taken out French citizenship, he got special permission from the English authorities to return for a short visit to Ireland in order to sell off his Cork properties. His brother had not been managing his estates well and O'Connor seemed frequently short of money. Immediately each new regime took power in France, O'Connor offered his services in the hopes of securing a better salary.

The general had three children, two of whom died young. His surviving son Arthur had two sons, Fernan and Arthur. Fernan joined the army, rose to the rank of general but never married. Arthur had two daughers, Brigitte and Elizabeth. Elizabeth had no children but Brigitte married Monsieur de la Tour du Pin and had three – Phyllis, a nun; Aymar, who married the Princess Maximilienne de Croy and has descendants, and Patrice.

Patrice de la Tour du Pin was a renowned poet during his lifetime but his popularity has waned since his death in 1975. There are many portraits of him in the château including one by Gerard and a fine sketch by Tchelitchef showing a long, thin and handsome, Irish-looking face. His widow says he appeared 'very Celtic' and wrote often about Ireland.

Brigitte O'Connor, the comtesse's mother-in-law, was the last with the general's name but mementoes of the family history are everywhere. Above the chimney-piece in the library hangs a life-size portrait of O'Connor wearing a red cloak and with his hand upraised. Underneath is a bust of Mirabeau.

The Irish Châteaux

Most of General O'Connor's retirement was spent writing and he published many pamphlets on social and political themes. He also helped to edit the works of his father-in-law, Condorcet. He died at the château in 1852 and is buried in the grounds.

The comtesse, her daughters and her grandchildren divide their time between the château and their homes in Paris. The estate land is let out to local farmers but the comtesse is a keen gardener and her work is much in evidence. To maintain the château, which is an expensive business, she is in the process of negotiating with the French authorities to have it proclaimed a literary landmark.

> In the war it was occupied by the Germans for three months but there was little damage. My husband was a prisoner-of-war for three years but my mother-in-law was living here. It is difficult to find things to do with a château because there are so many of them in France. It is historic and it could be consecrated to writers.

The comtesse also speaks of her husband's connection – the Paris-born Irishwoman, Madame de la Tour du Pin, *née* Henrietta-Lucy Dillon, who fled to America during the Revolution when her father, General Arthur Dillon (see Chapter Twelve), and her father-in-law, minister of war for Louis XVI, were guillotined during the Terror. In her memoirs, *Journal d'une Femme de Cinquante Ans*, Madame de la Tour du Pin, who was born in 1770, has left a fascinating account of what it was like to grow up at court during the reign of the ill-fated Louis XVI and his queen, Marie Antoinette, both of whom she knew. The journal, which has been widely read over the years, was translated into English by Felice Harcourt and republished in 1969. It was serialized on Irish national radio in 1989.

In it Lucy Dillon describes the confusion in the early days of the Revolution and the indolence, arrogance and ignorance of her class. She condemns the emigrés for abandoning France and leaving the mob to take control,

2: PORTRAIT OF O'CONNOR AND BUST OF MIRABEAU, LIBRARY OF BIGNON-MIRABEAU

3: LE BOUILH

4: PONT BELLANGER

and the officers for preferring to go abroad when threatened, thus allowing the NCOs to run the army. Separated from her husband, who as an aristocrat was on the run from the revolutionaries, she hid in Bordeaux with her two small children for several months during the Terror, short of food and hearing the daily drumrolls as heads tumbled from the guillotine. Eventually, with false passports secured through the help of Tallien, the Jacobin revolutionist sent to the city to quell opposition, the family escaped by boat to America.

Returning after several years to France, they then sought exile in England, but at the turn of the century her husband resumed his diplomatic career and served under both Napoleon and Louis XVIII. Madame de la Tour du Pin, who had an extraordinarily adventurous life, witnessing and surviving some of the most dramatic events in history, died in Pisa at the age of eighty-three. Only one of her seven children survived her.

The de la Tour du Pin family home was Château du Bouilh in the Gironde which was placed under seal during the Revolution. Madame de la Tour du Pin describes her return there from America in 1796 thus:

> I must admit that the first moments strained my courage to the uttermost. I had left this house well furnished, not perhaps in a

---

3   LE BOUILH *Fortress of the 14th century demolished* c. 1785 *by Comte Frederick de la Tour du Pin, who commissioned the architect of the Bordeaux Theatre, Victor Louis, to produce his most visionary design, dramatizing wine-making into an activity of Utopia. This design was modified in execution and interrupted by the Revolution. The comte's daughter-in-law, Lucy Dillon, mentions the house frequently in her memoirs. Now owned by M. Feuilhade de Chauvin.*

4   PONT BELLANGER *Medieval keep built by the Pont Bellangers and extended by them during the Renaissance. Linked in 1870 to a rival keep of bright red brick and joined by a corbelled turret to a circular tower. Interior dates from 1870. Restored after being damaged by both sides during the last war. Unique gothick shutters being replaced with replicas by the present Comte O'Mahony during time off from his farming.*

particularly stylish or elegant manner, but with everything in it comfortable and plentiful.

I returned to find it absolutely empty. Not a single chair was left to sit on, not a table nor a bed. I almost gave way to discouragement but to complain would not have helped. We set about opening the cases we had brought with us from the farm [in Albany, New York], for they had reached Bordeaux long before us, and the sight of the simple furniture in that vast house gave us much food for reflection.

The family managed to buy back some of the furniture that had been auctioned, including the collection of kitchen utensils destined for the Mint, and the library.

There is little of Lucy Dillon at Château de Bignon-Mirabeau. Her husband's family married into it later, and much of what she owned, including several Paris houses inherited from the Dillons, was lost in the Revolution or transported to America and sold in Boston.

An earlier family of Wild Geese who distinguished themselves in the French army over many generations were the O'Mahonys, today represented by a number of branches settled in the north of France. The head of the family, Comte O'Mahony, a retired officer of the French Foreign Legion, lives with his family at Château de Pont Bellanger in the Calvados district of Normandy.

The O'Mahonys of France are descended from Bartholomew O'Mahony, who was born in 1748 at Castleisland, Co. Kerry. He entered the Irish Brigades as a cadet in 1763 and later became a captain in Walsh's and a colonel in Berwick's regiment. In 1791, when Louis XVI was a prisoner in Paris, a large number of Irish royalist officers including the Duke of Fitzjames, the proprietor of Berwick's, Charles MacCarthy, its commander, and O'Mahony, its colonel, left France and joined the emigré princes and nobles at Coblenz who were intriguing with foreign powers for an invasion.

When the invasion was defeated at Valmy, for which the

republican force led by another Irishman, Arthur Dillon, got much of the credit, O'Mahony and other Irish Brigade officers, including Comte Walsh de Serrant, went to England to get help for the restoration of the Bourbons. They tried with some success to raise a regiment in Ireland for this purpose which they planned to incorporate in the British army, but it was sent to the West Indies instead. O'Mahony, however, joined the British army, became a colonel in Conway's regiment of foot and saw service in Portugal in 1804. He did not return to France until the Restoration in 1814 and was then appointed a lieutenant-general in the royalist army. He died in 1819.

Bartholomew O'Mahony had petitioned Louis XVI for letters of nobility and he was granted the title of comte. He had married Marie, daughter of the Marquis de Goury, and he left one son, Marie Yves Arséne, who was born in Paris in 1787. He too joined the army and lived first in Lyon, where he bought a château, and later in Switzerland. Although he had three wives who bore him eighteen children between them, only one of his children produced an heir, Maurice, who was born in 1881 and married Marthe Lafrete Damphernet de Pont Bellanger.

Maurice O'Mahony became a civil servant and lawyer in Orléans. He had 10 children but only two of the boys had children – Michael, father of the present comte, and Patrice. There are seven O'Mahony families descended from Bartholomew in France now, says the comte, and there will be seventeen in the next generation.

The comte is a retired army officer. He reached the rank of colonel and saw active service in Morocco and Indo-China. He was a prisoner of war in Vietnam for four years from 1950 and remembers it as the most awful period of his life.

The Vietcong did not take many prisoners; they let them die of malnutrition. We were kept in villages and were allowed only 600 grams of rice a day. What we needed most was salt. We had to boil the water to get rid of impurities. Proportionately more people died in the Vietnamese camps than in the Nazi camps.

Colonel le Comte O'Mahony was released following the Geneva Agreement of 1954. The following year he served with the French Foreign Legion in Algeria and was in Algeria again for the war from 1958-61.

Michael O'Mahony, the comte's father, also rose to be a colonel in the French army. A professor of tactics and strategy at the École de Guerre, he was wounded and taken prisoner at Dunkirk in 1940. He returned in 1947 to Pont Bellanger, which had been occupied three times by the Germans, and on the final occasion turned into a hospital. He died within the year.

Situated in the uplands of western Normandy, there was much action in the vicinity of Pont Bellanger. On one day in 1944 a battle was fought around the castle between the Germans and the Americans. Each held one side of the valley and they shot it out. While the work houses and stores were practically demolished, the château escaped surprisingly lightly.

Pont Bellanger had an earlier escape during the Revolution. The two sons of the house were in Coblenz with the emigrés, and a daughter was left alone. When the revolutionaries came to burn the château she stood at the window and said that if they set fire to the house they must burn her too. They withdrew and the heritage was saved.

The oldest papers relating to the château are dated 1182, but although it has remained in the one family and was never sold, despite changes of name through marriage, there is not a great deal of historical matter preserved, possibly because of its turbulent background. The stained-glass window over the portico was damaged by a bomb and the old tiles and a lot of furniture were stolen by each side in the last war. A family tree hangs in the library and a document published in 1790 in Nancy, for the purpose of explaining the letters of nobility, details Bartholomew's lineage from the ancient Irish family of Desmond and its attachment to Catholicism.

The Château de Pont Bellanger, where the comte and comtesse and, for part of the year, their five children live, lies in an almost secret valley in the heart of the lush Normandy countryside. Although a well-populated province, the area west of Caen is rural in the extreme. The château has a beautiful approach, down a straight avenue lined with trees. Most of the estate is rented out, but Colonel le Comte O'Mahony is busy maintaining the gardens and repairing the château which, because of its age, is constantly in need of renovation. His grandmother was the last of the Pont Bellangers and it is his responsibility, he says, as the eldest son of the eldest son and the head of the family, to maintain it and pass it on to his eldest son.

Two other O'Mahonys, who also came from Kerry, arrived in France a little earlier and had distinguished military careers. Richard Hayes writes of Daniel O'Mahony, who left Ireland after the fall of Limerick in 1691, having fought for the Jacobites, and who, as a member of the Irish Brigades, served in Italy where he is credited with saving the French forces from the surprise Austrian attack at Cremona in 1702. He was raised to the rank of colonel by Louis XIV and knighted by the Old Pretender. He then moved to Spain where he served in the armies of Louis's grandson, Philip V.

John Francis O'Mahony was son of Dermod O'Mahony of Dungloe, a colonel in Dillon's regiment. His son also joined Dillon's but as a royalist he left the French service in 1792 and eventually joined the Irish/English Brigade and fought against Napoleon in Egypt. He later returned to France and it was said of him, "He seems to have served with equal readiness for and against France, for and against the English, and under Bourbon, Napoleon and Orléans."

5: LA SORINIÈRE

TWO

THE LOIRE VALLEY – I

O'Kelly-Farrells, Brownes, Stapletons

O UTSIDE THE TOWN of Chemillé, south of Angers, hidden behind farm buildings and trees, lies one of the prettiest small châteaux imaginable. 'La Sorinière' is the home of the 8th Comte O'Kelly-Farrell, his wife and their seven children. Surrounded by a circular moat, the château is entered by a drawbridge hardly big enough and not strong enough to take a car, which leads to a fine courtyard, half gravel, half lawn. The back wall of the château drops straight to the moat; in the front a large tree gives shade to the lawn. Beyond the moat and among the outlying farm buildings is a thirteenth-century chapel.

'La Sorinière' has survived perfectly, despite two burnings. It has never been sold and has remained in the same family for nearly 800 years. Family crests on the walls of the chapel show the names of its owners – the de Pierres who built it about 1200, the de Brius, the d'Escoublants, the La Sorinières and the O'Kelly-Farrells. Each change of name came through the marriage of the heiress.

Denis O'Kelly was born at Clonlyon, Co. Roscommon, in 1715 and fought in the army of Spain. He returned to Ireland in 1740 to claim an inheritance from his maternal uncle, James O'Farrell, which necessitated adding his

5   LA SORINIÈRE *Built by the de la Sorinières c. 1280. Burnt out twice, the last time during the Revolution. Rebuilt 1805 with Georgian interiors inspired by the family's English exile. Drawbridge replaced by the present comte. Altar carved by his grandfather in frescoed chapel, which was filled with firewood during Revolution to escape destruction; now open to the public.*

uncle's name to his own. While away from France he married Mary Dillon of the Irish Brigades family and joined Prince Charles Edward Stuart (Bonny Prince Charlie) on his campaign in Scotland to regain the English throne.

Family papers at 'La Sorinière' state that he travelled with the prince to Eriska in the Outer Hebrides on Anthony Walsh's boat *Doutelle*, which left from Nantes in the summer of 1745. After the defeat at Culloden the following year O'Kelly-Farrell returned to France. In 1756 he received from Louis xv papers of French nationality and recognition of ancient nobility. He died in Toulouse in 1761.

Denis's son, Jean Jacques, was born in Dublin in 1749 and in 1786, having supplied the necessary papers, was given the title comte. Appointed a minister plenipotentiary by Louis xvi to the court of the Elector of Mayence, he was accused by the National Assembly in 1791 of associating with "the perfidious combination of armed Frenchmen" outside the kingdom. A staunch royalist, he resigned his post, lost all his property in the Revolution, and retired to Spain where he died in 1800.

Jean Jacques's son, the 2nd Comte, joined the emigré French nobles abroad and, like several Irishmen working for the Restoration, served in the British army. He died without children and the title passed to his brother Charles. The 4th Comte was Charles's son, Conor O'Kelly-Farrell, who died in 1915 leaving a daughter. The next comte was Conor's first cousin, Montrose Denis O'Kelly-Farrell, who died at the family château of Lansac, Merles, near Montauban in 1917.

Montrose's son, the 6th Comte, died in 1950 and the title passed to his cousin, Colonel James O'Kelly-Farrell, whose mother was Marie Thérèse du Verdier de la Sorinière. James's son, André, a captain in the French airforce, was killed in 1943 when his plane was shot down in Algeria. He was awarded the Croix de Guerre and, posthumously, the Légion d'Honneur. His son Jacques, James's grandson, is the current 8th Comte. He is an executive with the Renault car company and the land attached to 'La Sorinière' is let.

The O'Kelly-Farrells have a long record of service in the French armed forces. During the last century Malek O'Kelly-Farrell, father of James, served in Guadeloupe, the Crimea, Italy and Mexico. Other members were officers in various French campaigns in the Far East, including China, Cambodia, Laos and Vietnam, and in Africa.

The family's home from the end of the eighteenth century was Château de Lansac at Merles, now owned by cousins called d'Auterroches. 'La Sorinière', which came to the family on the marriage of Malek to the last of the Sorinières in 1875, has had a turbulent history. It was first burnt during the religious wars which swept through France in the sixteenth century and again burnt during the Revolution.

On each occasion the important tiny chapel, which is isolated from the château, survived because it was used as a wood store. Sixteenth-century frescos in the church, some of them depicting elephants which the artist had obviously never seen, have led to the building being declared a historic monument. There is a unique *pietà* with three figures above the altar.

The French Revolution was particularly bitter in this part of western France, La Vendée, and by 1793 a bloody civil war was raging between the forces of the republic and a Catholic-royalist army. An estimated quarter of a million people died. The church of St Pierre at Chemillé commemorates, in magnificent stained-glass windows, the arrest of Madame de la Sorinière and her sister-in-law, a nun, both of whom were guillotined in 1794. Described as a heroine of La Guerre de Vendée, this Madame de la Sorinière would appear to be the grandmother of the heiress who married Malek O'Kelly-Farrell.

One of the many Irishmen who fought for the royalists

in La Vendée and ended up losing his head was William Bulkeley, who had been born in Clonmel in 1766 and served in Walsh's regiment of the Irish Brigade. He joined the rebel royalist army under Charette but was captured, taken to Angers, and guillotined.

Richard Hayes lists several other Irish officers who fought with the royalists in La Vendée. They include Noel O'Byrne, who was saved from the guillotine by the revolution of Thermidor and the fall of Robespierre, and two other Vendéan leaders, O'Daly and Peter Dillon, who were not.

The O'Kelly-Farrells have a keen interest in Ireland despite being many generations removed from their country of origin and speaking little English. Several of their seven children have been given Irish names, including Scarlett, Patrick and Gael, which they say means an Irish emigré. The family have visited Ireland and their children have been on student exchanges with Irish children. A crest of Morogh O'Kelly, who died in 961, hangs in the library.

Another Franco-Irish family that travels frequently to Ireland are the Brownes of Kilmaine, who live in Tours. Their beautiful town-house is decorated with paintings, pictures, flags and other Irish memorabilia.

Kilmaine is a distinguished name in France because of 'le brave Kilmaine', the general who fought for France initially under the Bourbons, then with the Republic and finally for the Emperor Napoleon. Kilmaine was born Charles Edward Jennings in Dublin in 1751 but is known as General Kilmaine after the area in Co. Mayo of his father's land. His father was a doctor who settled in Tonnay Charente in the south of France in 1738, and his mother was Eleanor Saul of Saul's Court, Dublin.

Kilmaine was part of the French expeditionary force which assisted the Americans in the War of Independence

and on his return to France was a strong supporter of
the Revolution. He distinguished himself in defending the
Republic during the various invasions by European monarchs and emigré French nobles (among them many Irish)
that occurred in the early 1790s. He is particularly remembered for his bravery at Valmy and Jemappes. Despite being
appointed commander of the army of the north and saving
Paris by his retreat at Valenciennes, Kilmaine fell foul of the
reign of Terror and was imprisoned for several months as a
foreigner.

In 1796 he served in the Italian campaign with Napoleon
and was appointed commander of northern Italy. He was
picked to lead the planned French invasion of England
and Ireland which was later abandoned by the Directory.
Kilmaine was friendly with Wolfe Tone but was unsuccessful in his attempts to persuade the French government to
secure Tone's release from British custody by holding English hostages of similar standing in France. He died in Paris
in 1799 and left no heirs.

Henry Browne de Kilmaine does not claim relationship
to the general but his ancestor came from the same part of
Mayo, just outside Ballinrobe. His great-grandfather was
a younger son of James Caulfeild Browne, 2nd Baron
Kilmaine, who emigrated to France in the middle of
the nineteenth century, settled in Marseilles and married
a French woman.

> I think he left Ireland to study and then to buy land for his family
> but he died early and is buried in Pau in the Pyrenees.
> Our family originally came to Ireland from Lusignan, south of
> Poitiers, with William the Conquerer. They were Catholic but my
> great-grandfather, who was born in Dominick Street in Dublin,
> was a Protestant.

Monsieur Browne de Kilmaine is involved in the car business and is well known as one of the main organizers of the
Le Mans motor race. He has two sons and believes that the

three of them are the only people bearing the name, at least in France.

Interesting recent research by Fr Liam Swords of the Irish College in Paris suggests that the Empress Josephine's maternal grandmother was also a Browne from Co. Mayo. Born Josephine Tascher de la Pagèrie in Martinique, her mother was Rose Claire de Vergers de Sannois (1736-1807) and Rose Claire's mother was a Mademoiselle Browne whose family were from Co. Mayo. The connection was obviously known to Fr Jean Baptiste Walsh of the Collège des Lombards in Paris when he wrote to Josephine in August 1808, referring to Ireland as the home of her ancestors.

Farther down the Loire, between Tours and Angers, lies the ancient Château de Trèves which was bought by an Irishman, John Stapleton, in 1747, but passed out of the family shortly after he died in 1796. In a peaceful setting on the southern bank of the river, the Château de Trèves is today mainly one large tower, a ruined twelfth-century keep surrounded by a graveyard and enclosed by a low wall.

The Stapletons were originally from the townland of Drom, near Templemore in Co. Tipperary, where they were granted lands by King John of England and where the ruins of their castles remain.

The Stapletons have an interesting history in France. Walter Valentine Stapleton, whose two kinsmen, Colonel Stapleton, deputy governor of the city, and Mayor Purcell, were killed defending Limerick from the Williamites in 1691, left for France at the turn of the century and was naturalized there in 1717. He served for a time in the French West Indian colony of Saint-Domingue (now the island comprising Haiti and the Dominican Republic), where a cousin, Sir William Stapleton, was Governor of the Leeward Islands. As an officer in Berwick's regiment

Stapleton saw action in the War of Austrian Succession, and for gallant conduct at Fontenoy was promoted Brigadier des Armées du Roi.

Walter Stapleton accompanied Prince Charles Edward to Scotland in 1745 and commanded 400 soldiers of the Irish Brigade at Falkirk. He died in Nantes the following year from a wound received at Culloden and left six children.

Walter's cousin John, born in Limerick but whose family were from Thurlesbeg, Co. Tipperary, also lost his property as a result of supporting James II and he too, with his wife Helen Skerret, emigrated to Saint-Domingue. He came to France in 1704 and settled in Nantes where his son, John, Comte de Trèves, was born.

The title was given to John Stapleton by Louis xv in recognition of the family's loyal support for the Stuarts, and as well as the château he bought much of the surrounding land. French architectural sources state that Stapleton was not much interested in the old gothic building and within three years he had demolished the defensive wall. He is buried in the church attached to the tower.

One of John's descendants, Anne Stapleton, married the Baron de Segonzac, and although she herself was a victim of the noyades, her children survived. The noyades refers to the infamous method revolutionaries in Nantes employed to kill their enemies when the guillotines were too busy to cope with the demand; the condemned, mainly peasants taken in arms, were chained to great barges which were floated out in the river Loire and scuttled. During the Terror of 1793-94 thousands were dispatched in this manner. The Baron Hugues Louis de Segonzac of Château de Segonzac in Riberac is Anne Stapleton's descendant.

The château and land passed on John's death to his daughter Marie, who was married to J. B. Charles de Laurens, and after her through a multitude of hands. Today the Château de Trèves is the property of the local Départment.

6: Entry: Château de Serrant

THREE

THE LOIRE VALLEY – II

The Walshs

I N AN UPSTAIRS BEDROOM, not on view to the public,
in one of the grandest châteaux of the Loire, there are
seven small framed engravings of ruined castles in Ireland.
None of them stands today. They were in Co. Kilkenny and
they belonged to, or were founded by, the Walsh family.
The captions show them to be Castle Hoel (or Hoyle),
Knockmelon Castle, Courtstown Castle, Graces Castle,
Thomastown Abbey, Rosbercon Monastery and Grange
Castle.

The Château de Serrant, a national monument of France
some twelve kilometres west of Angers, is owned by a Bel-
gian, the Prince de Ligne. He inherited the château through
his great-great-grandmother, the Duchesse de la Tremoille,
born Valentine Walsh in 1830. Only one-sixty-fourth of his
blood is Irish, he says. Yet while the Walshs neither built the
castle nor possess it today, their mark is everywhere for they
owned it for more than 100 years from 1749.

The Prince de Ligne is a direct descendant, through
Valentine, of the 1st Comte Walsh de Serrant. The title
of comte (duc was added in Napoleonic times) passed to

6 SERRANT *One of the best-preserved châteaux of the Loire and one of
the few to have retained all its contents. Designed c. 1550 possibly
by Philibert Delormé, plans were completed by the Walshs when
they acquired it two centuries later, adding the axial entry arch
and flanking pavilions. They preserved the earlier interiors while
recording their assistance to Bonny Prince Charlie in an immense
portrait over the library chimney-piece. They also tactfully inserted
their own tombs into the chapel remodelled for the Vaubruns by
Hardouin-Mansart, architect of Versailles.*

the younger branch of the Walshs when Valentine's two nephews died in the middle of the last century. The present Duc de Walsh Serrant and his son, Charles Edouard, Comte de Walsh Serrant, live in less grand châteaux nearby.

According to V. Hussey Walsh, writing in the *Anglo-Saxon Review* of 1900, the Walshs of Serrant are a younger branch of the Walshs of Castle Hoel in Co. Kilkenny, who in turn are descended from Philip Walsh, one of the thirty-three knights who accompanied Strongbow to Ireland and obtained a grant of lands in the midlands in 1174. When his estates were confiscated by Cromwell in 1657, James Walsh of Ballynacooly, Co. Kilkenny, left home and joined the English navy.

After the battle of the Boyne in 1690 he captained the ship that took the defeated James II to his exile in France, and the Walsh connection with the Stuart cause began. It continues today in family names and is evident in the large painting (described later) which dominates the library at Serrant.

The son of this James Walsh, Philip, was born in Dublin in 1666 and when he was twenty-five he began business in St Malo as a ship-builder. Richard Hayes recounts that while he constructed several men-of-war for the French government, he augmented his fortune by engaging in the slave trade; Hussey Walsh adds that he aided the Stuarts by arming privateers and helping France fight England. Philip died suddenly in Madagascar in 1708 following an engagement with a Dutch vessel, and left five sons by his wife Anne White of Waterford and Clonmel. Three of the sons were later knighted and they are the forebears of today's Walshs of France.

Philip's son, Anthony, was born in St Malo in 1703 and having spent some years in the French navy set up a ship-building business in Nantes with sidelines in smuggling, privateering and slaving. In 1745 he was approached by Lord Clare, commander of the Irish Brigade, about a rising in Scotland to oust George II and regain the throne of England for the Stuarts. Walsh and another Irishman, Walter Rutledge of Dunkirk, who had been raiding English ships in the channel, agreed to provide two vessels, an 18-gun frigate and the 64-gun *Elizabeth*, captured from the English.

In a letter dated 12 June 1745, Prince Charles Edward wrote:

> Walsh understands his business perfectly well and is an excellent seaman. He has offered to go with me himself, his vessel being his own that I go on board of. He has also got a man-o-war that will go with me if she can be got ready in time and a frigate of 64 guns which he took lately from the English and is manning to be sent with the expedition. He lives at Nantes.

Walsh left Nantes with Prince Charles Edward on board the frigate *Doutelle* and he and George Kelly of Roscommon, Sir Thomas Sheridan of Cavan, Colonel John McDonnell of Fitzjames's regiment and Colonel John O'Sullivan of Kerry, were among the 'Seven Men of Moidart' who landed with the prince at Eriska in the Outer Hebrides in July 1745. The *Elizabeth* returned to Brest after a damaging encounter with an English man-of-war.

Once in Scotland, Bonny Prince Charlie raised his father's standard, the clans joined him and Edinburgh surrendered. He wrote to Walsh, who was returning to France:

> Notwithstanding what I have said to you by word of mouth I cannot let you leave me without giving you a written proof of the satisfaction with which I have received your services and I have asked the King, my father, to give you a striking proof of this.

The Chevalier, or Jacques Trois as many French still call him, consequently created Anthony Walsh, Earl Walsh. Appointed by Louis XV to command an expedition to Scotland, the project was abandoned after the crushing defeat at Culloden in April 1746.

The painting of Anthony Walsh and the prince landing in Scotland to start the rebellion hangs in the library at Serrant today. With the *Doutelle* in the background, Earl Walsh is depicted, as was customary at the time, as at least a foot smaller than the prince. While one Irishman had brought Bonny Prince Charlie to Scotland, it was another, Captain Richard Warren (see Chapter Nine), who rescued him from the Western Isles of Scotland where he had been forced to wander for weeks with a price on his head.

In 1753 Walsh's pedigree and noble birth were recognized by the French king and soon afterwards he went to the French colony of Saint-Domingue in the Caribbean to manage the family estates. He died there in 1763. Anthony, the 1st Earl Walsh, had married Mary O'Sheil, daughter of Luke O'Sheil and Anastase Galwey from the Cork Irish family, settled in Nantes, and they left several children. This senior line died out in 1884 with the death of the 4th Earl Walsh, who had lived at Château de Chaumont on the Loire east of Serrant.

Meanwhile the 1st Earl's younger brother, Francis, had been created Comte Walsh de Serrant by Louis xv in 1755. Born in 1704, Francis inherited a large fortune from his uncle, Patrick White of Waterford, which, according to Hayes, he increased by ship-building at Cadiz and slaving. In 1743 he married Mary Harper of Harperstown, Co. Wexford, and in 1749 he bought the Château de Serrant.

Francis's son, Anthony Joseph, the 2nd Comte Walsh de Serrant, served in the Irish Brigades and in 1774 he was involved in the strange plot, which Hayes recounts, involving Colonel Andrew MacDonagh of Dillon's regiment. MacDonagh had secretly married Rose Plunkett, daughter of Lord Dunsany, but in a row over an inheritance his wife was spirited away from her convent school in Lille and he was accused by Walsh of being a conspirator against the state. MacDonagh was imprisoned for 12 years on the Ile St Marguerite, off Cannes, where 'The Man in the Iron Mask' had just previously been incarcerated.

7: SERRANT: PORTRAIT OF ANTHONY WALSH AND PRINCE CHARLES
EDWARD AT MOIDART

8: Bouillé-Ménard

Released on the outbreak of the Revolution, MacDonagh, who was born in Sligo to a family that boasted forty immediate relatives serving in the Irish Brigades in France, successfully sued Walsh for his part in the affair and received 60,000 livres damages.

Anthony Joseph Walsh had by now become colonel-proprietor of a regiment but in 1791 he and many other anti-revolutionaries went abroad to join the emigré nobles in Coblenz. When the invasion of France failed at Valmy, Walsh and General Daniel O'Connell (uncle of the Liberator) turned to the English with the idea of raising several new regiments in Ireland as part of the English army, specifically for the purpose of fighting in France for the Restoration. This regiment ended up being sent to the West Indies.

The 3rd Comte returned to France on the establishment of the empire and received a number of titles from Napoleon. When the two comtes, Gaston and Ludovic, died young and without issue, one shortly after the other a hundred years ago, the magnificent Château de Serrant passed to their aunt, Valentine Walsh, wife of the Duc de Tremoille. The titles of comte and the newly acquired duc went to the descendants of Charles Edouard, second son of Francis, the 1st Comte.

The last Duc de Tremoille, Valentine's great-grandson, died aged twenty-two on a visit to England in 1933 when the castle where he was a guest caught fire (a scandal surrounded the circumstances of the tragedy in that the fire was rumoured to have been started by a jealous husband). Serrant then passed to one of his sisters, the Princess de

---

8   BOUILLÉ-MÉNARD *Built in the 14th century and extended in the 16th. Principal interiors were remodelled when acquired in 1770 by junior branch of the Walsh-Serrants. Sold and victorianized. Now restored by the present duke, who bought the château on hearing a mysterious command to do so during his mother's funeral.*

Ligne. Her son, whose home is in Belgium but who spends several months of each year at Serrant, is the present owner.

The prince is proud of his Walsh background and knows the family history well. Among the many documents, books and portraits at Serrant is displayed a small watercolour of a plain-looking ten-year-old girl in the gardens at Malmaison. This is Valentine, depicted when her mother, Louise de Vaudreuil, Comtesse de Serrant, was lady-in-waiting to the Empress Josephine. The empress was the child's godmother and her gift of china can be seen at Serrant today.

The Château de Serrant was first the home of the De Bries, an old Anjou family. Dating from 1546, it had a turbulent early history, including forced sales and occupations, before Francis Walsh bought it in 1749 from Madeleine Diana, wife of the Duc d'Estrées. Her portrait still hangs there.

The Walshs changed little in the château and avoided remodelling. They retained the mausoleum of the Marquis de Vaubrun in the private chapel, designed by Hardouin-Mansart and sculpted by Coysevox about 1700, and rather than rivalling it, incorporated their own.

The Walsh coat-of-arms, depicting a swan whose neck has been pierced by an arrow, is much in evidence at the château. It stands above the spectacular gate to the large inner courtyard and on its reverse is the letter W. When the Walshs bought Serrant this triumphal arch and the pavilions were their main additions. According to legend a swan helped a wounded Walsh across the Shannon and was then shot by the pursuers. The story is reflected in the family motto, 'Wounded but not dead.'

The Duc de Walsh Serrant, born in 1904, lives in the Château de Bouillé-Ménard, fifty kilometres away. It has been in the family almost continuously since 1770 and contains many Walsh memorabilia including the flag of the Walsh regiment. His title of duke, he says, is a Spanish one which came to the family from the Duchess de la Mothe d'Hourdincourt, whose mother was a Walsh, and it was recognized in France by Louis Phillipe.

He is sad that Serrant is no longer with his branch of the family but feels in any case that he would not have enough money for its upkeep. Before retirement he worked as a museum director in the Loire and has put much effort into restoring Bouillé-Ménard, which he bought back many years after his mother sold it.

He has done some research into the Irish regiments and tells how the Château de Serrant was saved during the Revolution. The wife of Anthony Joseph, the 2nd Comte and colonel-proprietor of Walsh's regiment, left alone as her husband fought with the emigré nobles abroad, welcomed the revolutionaries and gave them food and drink when they called. As a result they did no more damage than to take away two cannons.

The duke's son, Charles Edouard, the 10th Comte Walsh de Serrant, lives at Château La Maroutière, outside the town of Château Gauntier, north of Angers, where he farms about 240 acres, one-third of it cattle. He also breeds racehorses and has several in training. "It is hard to make a living as a farmer. A hundred hectares is not big, unhappily. The rest of the estate, three hundred hectares, is let out and in France we have horrible socialist laws and we cannot do what we want."

He is envious of the big estates of England where the inheritance does not have to be divided among all the children. He and the comtesse have four children: Marie Liesse, a striking tall teenager with red hair, a son studying in England and another in business, and a baby daughter. The comte does not expect either son to take up farming, although the duke has already willed Bouillé-Ménard to his eldest grandson, Ludovic.

La Maroutière, which dates from 1559, was inherited by his wife, Laurence, and had no connection with the Walsh family. To help with the upkeep of the château the comtesse takes in paying guests. She does not advertise but relies on recommendations. "It's a horrible house for a woman with all those stairs. My aunt had three maids when she lived here, now I only have a daily help," she says. Much work has been done in installing new bathrooms attached to the magnificent bedrooms and there are large grounds, a swimming pool and tennis courts. Two spacious cottages in the yard have been renovated, also for renting.

The comtesse is the area president of the organization Vieilles Maisons de France, and she recently arranged an exhibition of horrors of local architecture.

The comte was in Ireland only once, in the early 1960s. He and three cousins went shooting in Kerry. They bagged a large number of snipe and presented them to the proprietor of their hotel in Tralee. They waited two hours for them to cook and were dismayed by the burnt results. A happier memory is of marvellous wines discovered in the Kerry hotel. He and his cousins were so overjoyed that, for a laugh, they covered their heads with their napkins as they drank. The other diners took it to be a quaint French drinking custom.

He rarely shoots now. There is no game left in this part of France. Modern farming has seen to that. "How could a

---

9 LA MAROUTIÈRE 12*th-century castle burnt out during the Hundred Years War and rebuilt in flamboyant gothic. Carefully restored by the Comtesse de Walsh-Serrant's uncle, incorporating medieval doorcases from Bernay. Stone dormers include the device of the Walshs, a wounded swan.*

10 CHASSENON *A Louis-*XIV *château built on medieval foundations. Acquired by the Walshs and sold in 1800 to a Dane, M. Moller, who transplanted the most exquisite Renaissance fountain of La Vendée to the garden. Remodelled c. 1900 and inherited by M. and Mme de Kersabiec, both Walsh descendants. Recently acquired by their steward, M. Masson.*

9: La Maroutière

10: Chassenon

11: PLÉSSIS-MACÉ

JDW '09

partridge live here? Next door there is a farm with 4000 hens and the waste is spread on the land." Although there is some duck, the guns now are mainly for protection and there is one in every room. The comte is known as a good shot. The chief concern of most stately home owners in France are the Italian gangs who seek out valuable furniture. Guard dogs are everywhere.

The family have connections with several other châteaux in the region, including the Château de Chassenon where Patrick Walsh, another son of the original Dublin-born Philip, was established. It is rather run down now but stands in a magnificent setting next to a lake. An engraving of the events of 1789, when the mob came to attack the château, shows one of the Walshs preparing a meal for them and their quiet departure as a result. Until recent years the property was owned and lived in by the Kersabiec family who had married into the Walshs.

One of the most important medieval castles of the valley of the Loire, Pléssis-Macé near Château Gauntier, was also owned by the Walshs from 1749 to 1888 and is now the property of the Départment, who have opened it to the public and use it for a variety of events. It has a fifteenth-century keep surrounded by a twelfth-century wall and was extensively remodelled as a dwelling-house by Sophie de Walsh Serrant in 1868. It contains some family portraits.

---

11 PLÉSSIS-MACÉ 11*th-century château remodelled by the de Beaumonts in 1445 and abandoned in 1633 by the du Bellays, one of whom was the poet Joachim du Bellay, who immortalized the soft air of Anjou. Acquired as a ruin by the Walshs in 1749, the interior of the seigneurial residence was restored by Comtesse Sophie Walsh-Serrant in 1868. The Départment have recently replaced most of her interiors with an avant-garde exhibition centre, "again at our expense," one of her descendants observed, "this time as taxpayers".*

12: St Brice

FOUR

COGNAC

The Hennessys

MAURICE HENNESSY is seven generations removed from the Richard Hennessy who founded the famous cognac firm in 1765, yet he bears a striking resemblance to the handsome officer in the uniform of the Irish Brigades who, sword in hand, is portrayed around the world as the house symbol. Born in 1950, Maurice Hennessy is tall, elegant and charming in the way only a Frenchman can be, and he is director of one of the top five public companies in France, Moët Hennessy.

He is not keen that the firm should be so categorized:

> This is before the big denationalizing which we hope will come in a few years. The big groups have been nationalized by the socialists but when they are denationalized other companies will be much bigger than us. It is more important though that we are the biggest luxury item group in France.

Hennessy Cognac, established over two hundred years ago, merged with Moët et Chandon, the champagne company, in 1970 and since then have acquired the scent division of Christian Dior, Roc beauty products, a share in the Delbard Rose Nurseries and the Luxembourg Television network. More recently the Moët Hennessy group joined forces with Louis Vuitton, the makers of luxury leather goods, and Veuve Cliquot.

---

12 ST BRICE *A 17th-century château built over an immense range of cellars on the same level as the formal gardens linking it to the Charente. Later extension betrayed by slight irregularities of the fenestration. Garden vistas framed by geometrical box lead to a majestic fountain, a stag at bay defending his wounded mate from yelping hounds, with watching hounds spurting forth jets of water.*

Does all this mean that he is also very rich? "It depends. I do not like talking about these things; everything is relative." His uncle, also Maurice, has found a good way to describe the position. He told the 40th anniversary celebrations of Hennessy's L'Institut Social, a benevolent society run by and for the firm's employees, that when soldiers had won a war they tightened their helmets.

> We will have to start fighting again in order to win for the next 240 years. We have been successful because the people working for us have been hardworking and successful. We cannot say that tomorrow we will do as much.

That Jas. Hennessy and Co. is big business there is no doubt. In 1985 it had a turnover of 1.4 billion French francs but when all seventeen subsidiaries are included the figure was nearly double that at 2.46 billion French francs. There are two Hennessys who bear the name active in the firm and two who do not. The family, which has married extensively into the French aristocracy, is rich, powerful and famous. They own numerous châteaux, racehorses and treasures. They are Catholic? "Of course. We left Ireland for that; we are not going to change now."

Seven generations ago Maurice Hennessy's ancestor, Richard Hennessy, arrived in France from his home at Ballymacoy, near Mallow, Co. Cork. It was 1740, he was 26 years old, and he had come to join the Irish Brigades in the service of the kings of France. The family history recounts that while his father, Charles, was the local squire the property was not large and as the penal laws declared that a Catholic's land had to be divided equally among all the sons, rather than by primogeniture, many of the young Catholic gentry left for the Continent.

> The object of that brutal edict was to break up the land and therefore the position of the landed Irish families in the country. It was to avoid the disintegration of ancestral properties that the younger

sons emigrated. They were known at that time in Ireland as 'the
wild geese',

states a short family history which Maurice distributes to
interested parties. Ironically, the 3rd Lord Windlesham, Britain's Minister of State for Northern Ireland in the early 1970s, is
a Hennessy of Cognac. He headed the independent report on
the controversial 'Death on the Rock' television programme,
investigating the IRA deaths in Gibraltar in 1988, and cleared
the Channel 4 team of accusations of distortion.

Young Richard Hennessy joined Clare's regiment and was
based at La Rochelle, the main port of exit for cognac brandy.
He began to send casks home to friends, relatives and associ-
ates. The demand grew. He was injured in battle, and after
12 years retired from the regiment and moved to Cognac.
Old records dated 1765 indicate the creation of Hennessy,
Connelly and Co., in close correspondence with a firm called
Connelly and Arthur of Dunkirk. Ten years later, however, a
new firm was registered as Hennessy and Co. of Bordeaux.

By now Richard had married the widow of his first
cousin, James Hennessy of Ostende, with whom he had
stayed when he first arrived on the Continent. Ellen
Hennessy was a cousin of the statesman Edmund Burke.
Their son James, who was educated at the Benedictine
College of Douai along with other sons of Irishmen and
Jacobites living in France, gave his name to the fledgling but
expanding firm. To this day it is known as Jas. Hennessy
and Co. It is said that Jas., rather than James or Jacques,
embraced both names and could be more easily understood
by both English and French.

This Jas., who spent a short period in the Irish Brigades
early in life, was elected to the French parliament for the
constituency of La Charente several times during the reigns
of Louis XVIII and Louis Philippe. When the validity of his
French citizenship was challenged it was stated, according
to the *Journal des Debâts* of January 1825, that his father

had taken refuge in France because of his fidelity to James II and that the deputy himself, although born in Belgium, had been in France since he was three months old.

> Voting unanimously the admission of M. Hennessy, the Second Bureau was still divided upon the question as to whether M. Hennessy, the father, was actually a French citizen. After reading the letters written by Louis XIV and the Duke of Berwick as well as the edicts of Louis XV which declared as naturalized Frenchmen all the Irish (taking shelter by reason of their attachment to the cause of the Stuarts) who had taken service in France, the majority decided in the affirmative.

Jas. Hennessy married Martha Martell of the other big cognac firm and the couple had three sons, James, Auguste and Frederick. James took over the business while Frederick distinguished himself in hunting and founded a pack of hounds to hunt wolves. The pack has survived into this century although the quarry later became roe deer. James's son Maurice (1893-1905) introduced the star system for categorizing brandy.

Throughout, the Hennessy family have been involved in politics and several members have held parliamentary seats. M. Jean Hennessy (1874-1944) was variously minister for agriculture, French ambassador to Switzerland and candidate for the presidency of the Republic.

While there were arguments in the past about the nationality of the family, today there is no doubt that they are French. The name may be Irish but marriages through the generations have been with the French or the Spanish. Young Maurice Hennessy, whose grandfather, another Maurice, is the current head of the family, says he considers himself to be very much Irish.

> I feel Irish, particularly when I am in Ireland. I think like an Irishman when I am there. I have the blood very near the skin like an Irishman who gets excited and friendly. The Irish people like to be together. But it is difficult for me to describe myself. Some people tell me I am Irish. My grandmother who is from

Brittany tells me your grandfather is Irish of course. I always feel very much at home in Ireland.

Maurice Hennessy does not believe that the Irish connection has weakened with each generation. Nevertheless, while two of his aunts went to school in Ireland, none of today's children is being sent there. He has three daughters. "The French education system is complicated. Once you are out of it it is difficult to get back in. Maybe within the European Community this will change."

Maurice Hennessy goes to Ireland for four weeks every year on business. He is the landlord of the village of Killavullen, near Mallow, Co. Cork. The last descendants of Richard Hennessy's brother, Christopher, and his deaf and dumb sister, Olive, lived in the old house attached to the adjacent medieval castle of Monamy. But Christopher joined the diplomatic service and wished to sell the house.

> He wrote to my grandfather about it and we wanted to buy it, although the castle was a ruin. But it was during the war. It was difficult to communicate so we had no links with Ireland then; also de Valera's laws meant foreigners couldn't buy land in Ireland. It now belongs to someone else, I think. The real Hennessy home was destroyed in a nineteenth-century fire and any furniture or documents that existed relating to Richard were lost too. We wanted to buy even the stones but we were forbidden. The last things were a silver tray and a spinette which were in the keep at the beginning of the war but they had disappeared afterwards.

Maurice Hennessy bought another house built by the Hennessys near Ballymacoy, the ancestral home, on the other side of the river Blackwater, which he visits occasionally, but for a very busy high-powered business man he finds it rather remote. Ireland is his company's third largest market after the United States, to which Richard Hennessy first exported in 1794, and Japan. He generally visits Ireland for the annual Hennessy Literary Awards and the Hennessy Handicap, one of the many sporting events the firm sponsors.

There has been an equestrian tradition in the family

going back several generations, but Maurice is one of the few members who is not an avid racing enthusiast. His cousin, the Marquis de Geoffre, son of Isabelle Hennessy, is President of the French Racing Board.

Today business is good. In 1766 13,000 cases of cognac were shipped under the Hennessy name; by 1778 it had increased ninefold; in 1986 twenty-five million bottles were sold. Over time the firm has had more successes than reversals. Hennessys continued to operate throughout the Revolution but during the Napoleonic wars, when traditional commerce was paralyzed, most business activity was moved to Hamburg in Germany. During the cholera epidemic in England in the early 1830s consumption of cognac doubled because of the medical properties attributed to it.

When phylloxera attacked the Charentais vines at the end of the last century shipments fell by 60 per cent and the consequent increase in price had much to do with changing public taste; thereafter cognac was reserved for after dinner or for special occasions.

During the last war Cognac was lucky in that the German commandant appointed to the district, Otto Kleibisch, had been born and educated in the area and his family had owned a cognac company before the First World War. Consequently he was kind to the industry. He allowed production to continue, prevented the peasants who grew the vines being transported to labour camps, and ensured that premium prices were paid. As a result all the cognac houses profited from the Occupation and they were able to keep a vintage from each year which is vital for production.

The Hennessy distilleries and offices dominate the town of Cognac which naturally enough is the centre of the industry. Other prominent houses include Otard, originally Scottish Jacobites, and Martell and, in nearby Jarnac, Delamain and Hine. The Delamains were Huguenots who settled in Scotland before living for about one hundred years in Dublin.

They then moved to Jarnac where James Delamain married the daughter of the cognac-producing family of Ranson and in 1763 the firm became Ranson and Delamain.

While Otard, located in the stately Château de Cognac, the birthplace in 1492 of Francis 1, is the first distillery to be encountered entering the town from the north, it is Hennessy's huge warehouses, employing almost 900 people along both sides of the river Charente, that attract nearly 100,000 visitors a year. A navette, staffed by the green uniformed guides, brings the crowds, tourists and buyers from all over the world, back and forth across the river.

The family lives in several châteaux in the environs of the town. Kilian Hennessy, who was born in 1907 and is now retired, lives at the seventeenth-century Château de St Brice where he was host in 1980 to England's Queen Mother. Photographs of the visit hang at the plant's reception lobby. A renowned classical labyrinth or maze, four or five hundred years old, is a feature of the gardens.

In the family since 1830, but now company property, is the beautiful country house of Bagnolet situated about eight kilometres from Cognac amid rolling lawns and marvellous gardens that sweep down to the Charente. The exterior is neo-classical with a veranda like a New Orleans villa; the interior is Second Empire. The drawing-room opens into one of the few great nineteenth-century conservatories to have survived in France.

Important guests, many of them customers, are accommodated at Bagnolet when they visit the Hennessys and their distillery. It is magnificently furnished and fully staffed. Family portraits look over all proceedings and in pride of place hangs the picture of the Corkman who founded it all, Richard Hennessy.

13: LANGOA

JOU'

FIVE

BORDEAUX – I

Bartons, Lawtons, Exshaws, Johnstons, O'Quins, Phelans, Boyds, Kirwans, O'Byrnes, Clarkes

ANTHONY BARTON tells the story with pride. The Mayor of St Julien, the famous wine district in the flat feature-less Médoc outside the city of Bordeaux, has said that of all the châteaux in his Départment, the Bartons' Châteaux de Langoa and Leoville are the sole properties not to have changed hands in his lifetime.

The fact that the Bartons have been nine generations in Bordeaux since French Tom Barton left Ireland in 1722, and have always maintained close links with home (Robert Barton, a cousin, was a Sinn Féin signatory to the 1921 Treaty), makes them the leading Irish family in the district. But this was not always so. In the eighteenth and nineteenth centuries Irish names were commonplace among the grand trading and growing families. Some of those that have disappeared simply died out, or left the district, or lost the name through daughters' marriages, but in many cases the châteaux have retained the original Irish name and it is still seen on some of the finest wines in the world. In the city itself Irish surnames are found on buildings and streets.

---

13   LANGOA *Constructed by the de Pontets in 1758, acquired by the Bar-tons in 1821, who have maintained it as the least-altered 18th-century château of the Médoc, and the most perfect. Designed when servants were regarded as invisible, now adapted to when they no longer exist. A single range of first-floor reception rooms, with wine storage below, overlooks the entrance courtyard to the east and the gardens to the west, and links two pavilions, one for the family, the other for guests. Interior decoration reflects a change of taste from the rococo of the salon to the neo-classicism of the dining-room.*

In the Rev. C. G. D. Grimes's *Bordeaux and the English* (Ostend 1931) nearly two dozen of the families listed as prominent in the city in 1756 are Irish, and many of them, like the Lawtons, Bartons and O'Quins, are still there today while others such as Dillon, Boyd, Kirwan and Lynch are remembered on château-bottled wines. By the second half of the eighteenth century, when the Irish colony was at its height, there were between fifty-five and sixty Irish surnames in Bordeaux's merchant circles.

While some left with the Wild Geese, many were Protestants in flight neither from persecutions nor confiscations. Nor had they come to follow the Stuarts. With some exceptions, they did not join the Irish Brigades nor fight for the Bourbons. They sent wine, cognac and tea to Ireland, and the Bordeaux citizens – the most significant foreign group in Dublin in the mid-eighteenth century – sent wool, butter and beef back. The Irish in Bordeaux and the French in Dublin were intermarried, generally within religious lines, and there was constant travelling back and forth. Bordeaux has always been a busy port and a wealthy city. Even in the last war excuses are given for the paucity of the Resistance. Fighting, some natives say, was impossible since the land was too flat to have an underground.

While the Bartons are the most prominent Irish family, Château Boyd-Cantenac continues in business along with some of the other great names: Château Phélan-Ségur, Château Lynch-Bages, Château Lynch-Moussas, Château Dillon, Château Kirwan, Château Clarke and Château MacCarthy. The Mitchell glassworks, started in 1714 by a man from Cork, is still in existence.

The Bartons retained their châteaux and vineyards because they tended to marry foreigners and to keep their foreign passports, thereby making their own inheritance arrangements. Under French law, Anthony Barton explains, the property must be divided equally among direct descendants and this has caused the breakup of many estates and led to enormous legal complications and family feuds.

> One property here has just been sold because sixteen members of the family have inherited and they do not get on. It is very sad. We have maintained sole ownership because we have always been attuned to primogeniture. The Bartons have had English and Irish wives, not French wives. My wife is Danish and both my children were born in Copenhagen so that is how they are Irish. They have Irish passports like me. My father could have had his share of this but he agreed to take the Irish property instead.
>
> We are more Irish than French. We kept going back all the time since Hugh left France during the Revolution. I feel Irish although I was educated in England and have lived there for a large part of my life. We have got used to being a foreigner everywhere. It does not worry me in the least. I am not one of the modern generation who have to find themselves.

Anthony Barton is a handsome and charming man. Born at Straffan, Co. Kildare, in 1930, and educated first in Ireland and then at Stowe and Cambridge, he inherited Châteaux Langoa and Leoville Barton from his uncle Ronald. Cyril Ray, the English wine expert, has written that in the official listing by rank of the red wines of the Médoc, only two owners' names are the same now as they were in 1855, and neither is French – Rothschild and Barton.

> There has been a Rothschild at Château Mouton since 1852 but there has been a Barton at Château Langoa since 1821. Today no classified wine-growing château of the Médoc has been for so long in the hands of the same family as has Château Langoa-Barton, and Ronald Barton is the only grower to own both a second and a third growth.

The Bartons are an Anglo-Irish Protestant family. It is thought they came to Ireland from Lancashire with the army of the 1st Earl of Essex in 1573 and during the Ulster Plantation at the beginning of the seventeenth century settled at Curraghmore, Enniskillen, Co. Fermanagh. French Tom, a great-great-grandson of the first settler, left his home The Waterfoot on the banks of Lough Erne in 1722 at the age of twenty-seven. He set up first as a trader in Marseilles and then in Montpelier. Three years later he was in Bordeaux and trading French brandy and cognac for Irish wool, a business which was probably illegal in its initial stages.

By 1774 the Bartons of Bordeaux were the biggest buyers and shippers of fine clarets in the region, and they were rich. French Tom was one of the first Bordeaux shippers also to become a grower. He owned Château Le Boscq, no longer in the family, a country house at the sea, and The Grove at Fethard, Co. Tipperary, now owned by a branch of the family, the Ponsonbys. When he died he left his six grandsons £10,000 each. The French and Irish estates and the Bordeaux business went to his only son, William.

One grandson, Hugh, eventually took over the business and married Anna Johnston, daughter of another Anglo-Irish Bordeaux family. In the Reign of Terror of 1793 the Bartons, the Johnstons and many other foreigners were detained as prisoners in the former Carmelite Convent. Their fellow prisoners included about forty clerical students from the Irish College in the city, among them the 1798 leader Fr Murphy of Wexford. Lacombe, the dreaded president of the Military Tribunal, took the College itself as his headquarters, and guillotined its superior, Fr Martin Glynn.

Hugh Barton escaped and family folklore has it that he took the keys of the guillotine with him. The macabre contraption was of course named after its inventor Dr Guillotin, who, strangely, had been a teacher at the Bordeaux Irish College before the Revolution. It is said he offered his invention as a more humane way of chopping off heads than the customary axe.

Making his way to Ireland, Hugh left the business in the hands of his partner, Daniel Guestier, and thus was born the firm of Barton and Guestier, an association which was to survive until 1956. Hugh stayed first with his brother in Fethard and then bought Straffan House. Having consolidated his Irish and English businesses he returned to France ten years later. He is reputed to have made a huge fortune immediately after the Napoleonic wars, and in 1821 he bought Château Langoa, castle and vineyard, from Monsieur Bernard de Pontet. Five years later he purchased part of the Leoville estate, which had been confiscated from the Marquis de Lascases when he joined the emigré nobles abroad.

The vast Leoville property, once the biggest in the Médoc, is now divided into Leoville Lascases (60 hectares), Leoville Poyferré (36 hectares plus the château), and Leoville Barton (35 hectares). The Langoa and Leoville wines have always been kept separate and neither is connected with the Barton and Guestier shipping partnership.

Hugh Barton saved his business during the Revolution by leaving Guestier in charge, and 150 years later history repeated itself. Ronald Barton, brought up at Straffan but educated at Eton and Oxford, called upon the descendant of the Guestier who saved his great-great-grandfather's firm to do the same for him.

In 1940, as the Germans approached Bordeaux, Ronald Barton fled to England, joined the Royal Inniskilling Fusiliers and served as a liaison officer with the Free French, first in England, later in the Middle East and North Africa. He was awarded the Légion d'Honneur, the Croix de Guerre, the Medaille Commemorative de la France Libre, and the CBE.

Daniel Guestier meanwhile persuaded the Germans that the whole property – château, furniture, vineyards and full cellars – were owned by an Irish neutral. Ronald's sister, who was an Irish citizen living in Ireland, contacted the German authorities through the Irish Legation in Vichy and demanded that the property be untouched. All was saved, although the Germans took over Château Langoa as a billet. When he returned in 1945 Ronald had many years of hard work in building up the neglected vineyard to its former reputation, and he did so without the wholesale replanting of new vines to which other owners resorted. He died in his garden at Langoa aged eighty-three in 1986.

Today the wine business is good. Many châteaux, long neglected, are being restored for the first time in thirty or forty years. "Wines at this level have only become profitable in the last fifteen years," says Anthony Barton. Château Langoa is also being done up. When his father, Derick, sold the magnificent family home, Straffan House, in 1937, its contents were dispersed. Much of the furniture was Louis xv, bought in France by generations of Bartons.

Anthony Barton is anxious to recover some of the furniture, paintings, silver and china. He responded to an advertisement in *The Field* and two Lowestoft chinese plates with the Barton crest were found in Dallas, Texas. "They are now here at Langoa and I am sure they cost me much more than they did in 1937. But the two plates from the whole 1750 dinner and dessert service is all we have." He refused to say what he paid for them in case it might upset his parents who still live in Dublin.

There is little of Irish interest now at Langoa apart from family portraits, as most furniture tended to go the other way – from France to Ireland. A painting of the start of the 1872 Conyingham Cup at Punchestown hangs in the office. The search for items from the Straffan sale continues.

While the Bartons kept their Irishness, other Anglo-Irish families who emigrated around the same time have become French in all but name. Hugues and Daniel Lawton are seventh-generation Irish and are two of the most respected wine businessmen in Bordeaux. Hugues, the elder, is a *négotiant*, or agent, and Daniel is a broker, Gaullist city councillor for the past twenty-six years, deputy mayor of the city and former sports star in hockey, tennis and golf. Few visitors to Bordeaux with any interest in wine can leave without encountering one or both of the brothers. They are witty and knowledgeable hosts with a fund of anecdotes going back several generations.

Hugues Lawton says his ancestor, Abraham Lawton, was born in Cork in 1716 and arrived in Bordeaux in 1739. The family is believed to have come from Lawton Hall in Cheshire where they were known during the time of Henry IV of England. They crossed to Ireland with William of Orange and founded a branch at Lake Marsh, now known as Lough Mahon, on the estuary of the Lee. A Hugh Lawton was Mayor of Cork during the 1770s and the family have a sketch of what they believe was his statue.

Hugues Lawton has been to Ireland often yet is unable to trace any existing family connection or where, other than the name Lake Marsh, the family came from. "We would like to know more. There is always a great question mark. It is a failure of some of our ancestors. We do not know why they left Cheshire or why they came here to Bordeaux."

Abraham Lawton lived at 43 Cour d'Arnozan, which is set into one of the finest architectural set-pieces of Bordeaux rococo. He set up in business at the Quai des Chartrons, where the brothers still have offices in the old buildings facing the railway line and, beyond that, the Gironde. England and France were at war at the time and business was good for those who could ship wine into England through Ireland.

> Enormous quantities of wines were shipped to Ireland and it is impossible that they were all for the Irish market. We think they were smuggled into England.
> Some of the Irish never became French, such as the Bartons, but we became French very quickly. Abraham fell in love with a French girl but because he was a Protestant and a foreigner her parents

were afraid for her and it was only after they had several children that they were allowed to marry. But we are very attached to our Irish origin and proud of our ancestry.

The only thing I can say is that we have a diary of Abraham's grandson, Edward, who was born in 1795, and he tells the story, half in English, half in French, of how in spite of the wars he managed to get back and forth to Ireland. In the middle of the Napoleonic wars he writes, 'I am leaving Bordeaux with Johnston, Barton and MacCarthy and we go to Helgaland to pick up some passports and we get ships going into London and then proceed to Bath and to Ireland.'

Hugues continues:

We are the oldest wine brokerage business in the city and we are still in the same offices. My brother still writes a journal every day – the weather, business, political events. The woman who wrote *La Bicyclette Bleu* about the Resistance came to him to check on the weather.

In 1944 my cousin Jean Lawton went to Britain with wine which he wanted to swap for weapons for the underground movement. Bordeaux had been liberated from the Germans at this stage but they still held the mouth of the river. He was sent because he could speak English and I think in a way he succeeded although at first he was put in a camp for questioning as a spy.

The family has only occasionally produced wine. The brothers' grandfather, Edouard, owned Leoville Poyferré through his wife for a mere twenty-seven years around the turn of the century, but the Lawton crest remains on the bottle. Their cousin Jean bought Château Cantenac Brown in 1935 and sold it in 1968. Hugues feels it is a bad idea for a wine broker to have an estate: "You can get squeezed." In any case their father was more interested in politics. He was influential in having Jacques Chaban Delmas, who later went on to be Prime Minister of France, elected mayor of the city.

Abraham Lawton's order book is in Daniel's office. During the year 1764 business was done with people by the name of Nally, O'Byrne and MacCarthy, and there were shipments to Galway. After the Revolution entries were in French rather than in English but the names of Phelan, Lynch and others from Ireland appear frequently.

Most of the old family documents, including one showing that a witness at the wedding of William Lawton in 1790 was Eleanore Sutton de Clonard MacCarthy of an Irish Brigade family, are in the apartment of the brothers' mother, Madame Simone Lawton (*née* de Luze in 1897) on the Cours de Verdun. She is frequently consulted by researchers and remembers the time when the grand families had their town houses or hotels. The elusive Hôtel MacCarthy she could pinpoint instantly.

At Madame Lawton's we met Guy Exshaw. His ancestor, John Exshaw, born in Dublin in 1782, came to Bordeaux around the turn of that century and in 1816 married Suzanne Corine, daughter of Pierre François Guestier of the wine family, and of Jane Hoey, who was born in Dublin in 1772. Jane Hoey was married in 1793 and witnesses at the wedding – Guy Exshaw still has the document – included Johnstons and Lynchs. Her sister Elizabeth had married Lord Talbot the previous year.

Monsieur Exshaw also has in his possession a second edition of Smollett's *Travels through France and Italy*, which was printed in Dublin in 1772 for, among others, J. Exshaw, J. Hoey jun. and E. Lynch. The name G. Galwey is written in old-fashioned script on the flyleaf.

The Exshaws were one of the few Irish families in France who actually built a château instead of buying one or, more frequently, marrying into one. Frederick Exshaw in 1880 built Château La Chesnaye-Ste-Gemme in the Médoc. This immense Victorian pile, now empty and no longer owned by the family, is an imposing sight.

The Johnstons, who appear constantly in the history of wine in Bordeaux, were so grand at one stage that they even had their own compound 'L'Enclos Johnston' on the Chemin de Mougnac. They are reputed to have given the largest private balls in the district at a time when the Irish community, including wives and children, numbered about 300 persons. The main house, Lescure, bought by Nathaniel Johnston in 1810, is now the deaf and dumb hospital at Place des Cèdres.

The family came from Scotland to Ireland around 1640 and settled at Gilford, Co. Down, and Kilmore, Co. Armagh. William Johnston is credited, in the family history, with having constructed the cathedral of Armagh and one of the bridges over the Lagan in Belfast. He was killed at the siege of Derry in 1689, fighting on the Williamite side.

The first Johnston to move to France was another William, who left Ireland about 1800 and set up in business in Bordeaux. The family was highly successful and Nathaniel, at different stages, owned the beautiful Château Lascombes and Château Dauzac in Margaux, a share in the renowned Château Latour in Pauillac with Barton and Guestier, the magnificent Château Ducru-Beaucaillou in St Julien and the town-house Lescure.

By this time they had become French in all but sur-name, having taken out citizenship and converted to Roman Catholicism. Business problems that followed the introduction of Prohibition in America forced Nathaniel to sell Ducru-Beaucaillou, to which he had added two square towers in 1928 after seventy years of ownership. The buyer was Monsieur Desbartats de Burke. The Johnstons are still highly regarded *négotiants* in Bordeaux.

---

14 DUCRU-BEAUCAILLOU *Originally a long one-storied 17th-century wine store, topped with an elegant neo-classical pavilion by Bertrand Ducru in 1795. Acquired from his daughter in 1866 by the Johnstons who victorianized the interior and added a swaggering tower at each end. Owned 1928-41 by M. Desbarats de Burke whose grandchildren now own Châteaux Siran and Pichon Lalande. Restored by the present owners, M. and Mme Jean-Eugène Borie.*

14: DUCRU-BEAUCAILLOU

JDW '88

15: ABRAHAM LAWTON

16: MME LAWTON

17: CHESNAYE-STE-GEMME

A Jacobite family that is still prominent in Bordeaux is the O'Quins and one of them, Henry O'Quin, recently published a detailed book on the family history, which starts in the second century. The first O'Quin to come to France was Patrice, whose mother was a Joyce and who was born in Ballinrobe, Co. Mayo, around 1679. He took up the Stuart cause and followed James II to his exile in St Germain-en-Laye. He moved later to Bordeaux where he became master of shipping in 1704 and married Jeanne Lee, daughter of an Irishman. His brother André travelled the world and the family in general was much involved with colonial traffic.

In 1793 a Patrick O'Quin was 'commissaire du Conseil General de la Commune', and several years later Antoine Patrice O'Quin was given the title of comte by Louis XVIII. The family has since achieved high rank in the army and navy and today holds important positions in the port of Bordeaux.

Of the Irish families that have vanished from the area the most distinguished were the Lynchs, Dillons and MacCarthys, dealt with elsewhere in this book. While Château Phélan-Ségur is still in St Estèphe, the Phelans themselves have gone. Originally from Tipperary, they settled in Bordeaux at the end of the eighteenth century. Bernard Phelan bought Château de Ségur in 1810 and passed it on to his son Frank when he died in 1841. Frank had married one of the Guestiers and their three daughters sold the property in 1918. Their descendants are now dispersed throughout France, where one is the Baron Turckheim and another the Comtesse Roland de Quatrebarbes.

---

17 LA CHESNAYE-STE-GEMME *Built in 1880 for Frederick Exshaw by architect M. Garros. Possibly the only château built by an Irishman in France, albeit as a French version of an English castle. Vast, grim, explicably abandoned.*

There is no Boyd either at Château Boyd-Cantenac, which produces some of the finest wines in the region. The owner, Pierre Guillemet, is anxious to help those seeking the Irish link, but his knowledge is sketchy. It is known that Jacques Boyd, of Belfast origin and married to a Barton, purchased the property in 1754 and gave it his name. The couple lived in the city as there has never been a château attached to the vineyard and *chais* (wine store).

Jacques went bankrupt in 1782 and his son, George, followed the same course seven years later. There was a wave of bankruptcies during the decade and as well as the Boyds, the Gernons, O'Byrnes, Gledstanes and Galweys all failed. Although one Barton partnership collapsed, William Barton did not, and in 1788 he surprised all his colleagues by buying up all the Lafite, Latour, Haut Brion and Château Kirwan in the district for upwards of 460,000 livres.

The last Boyd, a Mademoiselle Skinner, married into the nearby Browns, who were Scottish, and lived at Château Brown-Cantenac. The Browns, who had taken over the vineyard, in turn went bankrupt in 1841 and the Guillemets, who live on their other property, Château Pouget, bought Boyd-Cantenac in 1932.

One of the most beautiful château in all of the Médoc, where behind every clump of trees hides a castle, is Château Kirwan in Margaux. It is now owned by the Société Schröder et Schÿler but wine was made on the estate as early as the twelfth century. In 1715 it was bought by Sir John Collingwood, who is described sometimes as English and sometimes as Irish. One of his two daughters married Mark Kirwan from Galway, a wine merchant of Bordeaux, and he eventually inherited the château and vineyards.

Before he was guillotined during the Revolution, Mark Kirwan changed the name of the property from the ancient Domaine de Lassalle. His son Edward was also imprisoned for his royalist views, but he managed to keep his head and went on to become editor of a local paper before, it is believed, eventually returning to Ireland. After the Restoration Mark Kirwan's children regained Château Kirwan and during the early part of the nineteenth century a Mademoiselle Kirwan was running the property.

The O'Byrne family was also in Bordeaux in the mid-eighteenth century although not mentioned by Grimes in his list. John O'Byrne of Cabinteely, Co. Dublin, emigrated to France at the beginning of the century with several members of his family and bought Château La Houringue at Macau. He married Mary Gernon, of a family who had come to France from Gernonstown, Co. Louth, and in 1770 he and his two brothers, Gregory and Daniel, got letters of nobility from Louis xv. The brothers' mother was Mary Anne Colclough of Wexford and the archives show that their uncles, Barneval and Colclough, were both officers in Berwick's regiment of the Irish Brigade and that the latter died of wounds received at Fontenoy.

John O'Byrne was called 'The Chevalier O'Byrne of La Houringue' and one of his sisters married Edward Kirwan, the newspaper editor. Today La Houringue's vineyards (the large O'Byrne estates were sold at public auction when the family joined the emigrés during the Revolution) are part of the Château Giscours estate, but the house itself is still lived in and is clearly visible, surrounded by trees and across acres of vines. Outside the walls are covered in ivy, and inside in silk; the *belle époque* decoration has been retained.

At Château Clarke in Listrac there is neither château nor family. It is known, however, that Irish Jacobites called Clarke from the area of Dromantin, Donaghmore, Co. Down, came to France after the Boyne, and bought the estate in 1771.

Tobie Clarke was originally an arms-dealer (*armateur*) in Nantes before moving to Bordeaux and his eldest son, Luc-Tobie, a judge in the criminal court of Bordeaux, who was imprisoned for a time during the Revolution, gave the château its name in the early part of the nineteenth century. On his death in 1818, however, his children being minors, the château and the large estate of 232 hectares were sold by the state to the Saint-Guirons family, who retained it until 1955.

The château was then demolished by its new owner, a Monsieur Bidon. Today Château Clarke is the centre of a vast estate, 177 hectares, owned by Baron Edmond de Rothschild, who bought it in 1979 and joined it to Château de Peyrelebade. With the exception, of course, of the highly prized vines, all that remains of the original Clarke estate is the name and a pair of ornate iron gates leading up a long avenue to a collection of warehouses.

The family Clarke de Dromantin is well established in the city of Bordeaux and one of them, Patrick Clarke de Dromantin, is currently engaged in research on Irish families in the area.

---

18   CHÂTEAU PHÉLAN-SÉGUR *18th-century château acquired and extended by Bernard Phelan and his wife, Marie-Elizabeth Guestier. Remodelled in ponderous Italianate by their son Frank on his marriage to Wilhemine Guestier in the mid-19th century.*

19   CHÂTEAU BOYD-CANTENAC *18th-century house attached directly to its chais; when the door is opened between them, a sudden smell of wine permeates the interior.*

20   CHÂTEAU KIRWAN *Built for Sir John Collingwood in the mid-18th century and called the Château Lasalle, it was inherited and renamed in 1781 by his son-in-law, Mark Kirwan. Sold by the family in 1827, it has been restored by Mme Jean-Henri Schyler, wife of the present owner.*

18: PHÉLAN-SÉGUR

19: BOYD-CANTENAC

20: KIRWAN

21: LYDE

22: LYDE, THE SALON.
PORTRAIT OF COMTE LYNC[
BUSTS OF LOUIS XVI
AND OF HENRI III

SIX

BORDEAUX – II

The Lynchs and the Burkes

T HE STORY OF COMTE LYNCH is continually told in Bordeaux. For many, Lynch is a byword for expediency and the ability to swing with the political pendulum, and to get away with it, which has made the city the great centre of wealth and prosperity it is today.

Jean Baptiste Lynch, Mayor of Bordeaux, was the French-born grandson of an Irish emigrant, Colonel John Lynch of Cranmore in Galway, who had followed the Stuarts to France after the defeat of the battle of Aughrim in 1691 – "par attachement pour ce prince et pour conserver le libre exercise de la réligion catholique". He set up business as a wool and leather merchant and married a French woman. His two sons also prospered and, having sufficient money, they successfully petitioned Louis XVI to be admitted to the French nobility, contending that they came from such stock in Ireland and that their papers had been confiscated.

Born at Château Dauzac in the Médoc in 1749, Jean Baptiste was initially an enthusiastic parliamentarian and a champion of independence from the Crown. Once the Revolution was underway, however, he started his habit of switching sides whenever it became necessary, and it is for this that he is best remembered.

Regarded as an enemy of the Revolution because of his

---

21 LYDE *Built in 1632 to a grand design in miniature round three sides of a courtyard, a tower on a central axis over the entrance and towers at each corner. Acquired by Olivier Garaud's father and carefully restored in homage to the Bourbons.*

letters of nobility, and in an attempt to preserve his vineyards, châteaux and estates, he abandoned his commitment to parliament and became a zealous royalist. It was a time of unprecedented turbulence and his action in adopting whatever was politic for the day was not as unusual as it seems in retrospect. For him, though, it was only the first of many such moves.

This first turnabout, his adoption of the royalist cause, led to his imprisonment during the Reign of Terror in 1793 and the confiscation of his property. Released on the fall of Robespierre, he recovered his lands the following year and after some time in politics he became Mayor of Bordeaux in 1809. Although a Bourbon supporter, he headed the delegation from France's second city at the marriage of Napoleon to Marie Louise of Austria in 1810, and once there made the first of many public professions of loyalty to the emperor, for which he received the title of comte.

In January 1814 Lynch offered the help of the people of Bordeaux to Napoleon, whose difficulties were mounting. But in March, when the English General Beresford, a natural son of the 1st Marquis of Waterford, and his army, ostensibly in support of Louis XVIII, approached the city, from which the Bonapartists had fled the previous night, he was welcomed in by the mayor. Lynch is reported to have thrown down his tricolour ribbon and Napoleonic insignia and replaced it with the white cockade and scarf of the Bourbons.

When the Duc d'Angoulême, Louis XVIII's nephew, arrived, he and his wife, the only daughter of the executed Louis XVI, were given a triumphal reception by the mayor. The citizens were greatly surprised by this volte-face and Napoleon never forgave Lynch for his action at such a crucial time. When he returned from Elba the following year the ex-emperor said that he pardoned everyone except his two greatest enemies – Comte Lynch and the royalist Laine.

Lynch fled before Napoleon could carry out his threat to shoot him. He and the Duchesse d'Angoulême, who had delayed as long as possible in Bordeaux and was described by Napoleon as "the only man among the Bourbons", embarked at Pauillac on a boat for England. There Lynch was honoured and fêted by the English and by the French emigrés as a hero of the Restoration, and presented to the Prince Regent. He abandoned his plans to visit Ireland when more pressing events on the Continent demanded his attention.

Napoleon was defeated at Waterloo. Lynch returned to France and was awarded the designation Peer of France on the second restoration. He continued for several more years in public life but retired following the July Revolution of 1830, which brought Louis Philippe of the Orléans Bourbons, to the throne. He died in 1835 at Château Dauzac, aged eighty-six.

While the Lynch name is gone – neither Jean Baptiste nor his brother Michel left heirs – it is still much in evidence on the finest bottles of wine from the Médoc and there are descendants of the brothers' sisters and of their uncle Jean Jacques Lynch. In the late 1930s a Mademoiselle Lynch lived in Bordeaux, a descendant of the comte's cousin. She was a Protestant schoolteacher and the last to bear the name.

Château Lynch-Bages, Château Lynch-Moussas and Château Dauzac were the main Lynch properties. Lynch-Bages came into the possession of Thomas Lynch, the comte's father, when his brother-in-law, Pierre Drouillard, died in 1749. The family kept the château and vineyard until they were sold in 1824.

Today Lynch-Bages is the property of the Cazes family, who bought it in 1934. André Cazes was Mayor of Pauillac for many years and the old house has been entirely renovated and modernized. His son Jean-Michel is proud of the Irish link and frequently entertains visitors from Ireland.

The Irish Châteaux

Château Lynch-Moussas has been in the hands of the Casteja family since 1919 and in the early 1970s the two families, Cazes and Castejas, went to court to prevent the then owner of Château Dauzac, M. Alain Miailhe, adding the name Lynch to the title of the wine. M. Miailhe, who claims descent from the Lynchs on his father's side and whose mother was a Burke, argued, with justification, that Château Dauzac had more connections with Comte Lynch than the other châteaux that bore the name. M. Cazes said:

> We thought it was not fair; it was not a well-known estate. We won and it has gone back to being Château Dauzac again. We did not mind if he had put on the bottle 'ancient property of Comte Lynch' but he couldn't call it Château Dauzac Lynch.

From 1863 to 1920 Dauzac belonged to another Irish descendant, Nathaniel Johnston (see Chapter Five), and it was during his time at the château that the famous 'Bordeaux Mixture' for fighting mildew on the vines was discovered. Alain Miailhe bought the property in 1966 but was forced to sell it eleven years later because of the only too common French inheritance problems. It is now owned by the Chatellier family.

---

23 CHÂTEAU DAUZAC *Early 18th-century château known as La Bastide, acquired and renamed by Thomas Lynch. Here his celebrated son, Jean-Baptiste, was born in 1749 and died nearly ninety years later. Owned by Nathaniel Johnston from 1863 to 1920 and later by Alain Miailhe, who resold it unrestored when he was refused permission to rename the wine Lynch-Dauzac. Now derelict.*

24 CHÂTEAU LYNCH-BAGES *Estate inherited by Elizabeth, wife of Thomas Lynch, from her brother Pierre Drouillard. Lived in by her younger son, Michel, who managed it for his elder brother, Jean Baptiste. Sold in 1824 to a Swiss, Sebastiane Jurine, who built the present château. Acquired by the Cazes family in 1914 and now being restored and extended by them.*

25 CHÂTEAU LYNCH-MOUSSAS *Elegant 18th-century château acquired by the Lynchs and owned in the mid-19th century by a Spaniard called Vasquez, when it was fancifully extended. Restored by the present owners, M. and Mme Émile Casteja.*

74

23: DAUZAC

24: LYNCH-BAGES

25: LYNCH-MOUSSAS

26: SIRAN

JDW '89

27: PICHON-LALANDE

JDW 89

Alain Miailhe and his sister, Madame de Lencquesaing, own and run two of the great châteaux of the Médoc – Château Siran and Château Pichon-Longueville, Comtesse de Lalande, respectively. They are one-quarter Irish, or possibly slightly less. Their grandmother was the daughter of a Burke from Galway who had married a Spanish Filipina. Despite their paternal descent from the Lynchs, a rather remote connection, their Irish blood, which in Bordeaux terms is very recent, has led to a great interest in Ireland and all things Irish.

M. Miailhe has written on the Lynchs, the Burkes and the Irish generally, and has collected documents, published pamphlets on the subject and researched such relevant areas as the Irish Brigades. One of the few portraits of Comte Lynch hangs in the drawing-room of his *chais*, but it is a copy made in the Philippines from the original in the city hall of Bordeaux.

A family tree, entitled 'Pedigree of the Burkes of Clanricarde', which starts at Pepin who died in 768, is on display in his office. He has pinpointed his line and argues that the title and property of the Clanricardes should have gone to his grandmother's brothers. "We were much closer than the Lascelles but we were Catholic and it was a question of religion." Because of this connection he was offered the ruined Clanricarde Castle of Portumna by the Irish Board of Works on condition that he was prepared to restore it at his own expense. He declined.

---

26 CHÂTEAU SIRAN *18th-century château built by the de Bosqs and inherited by Comtesse Alphonse de Toulouse-Lautrec, great-grandmother of the artist. Sold in 1848 to the Miailhes and restored as the most Palladian château in the Médoc. Collection of contemporary sculpture above ground, a nuclear bunker stacked with wine beneath.*

27 PICHON-LALANDE *Built c. 1840 by the widowed Anne-Laure, Comtesse de Lalande, youngest daughter of Baron Pichon-Longueville, who lived across the road. Her lover the Comte de Beaumont gave her the site and subsequently commissioned her architect, Duphot, to design Latour.*

John and Richard Burke were two Galway brothers who settled in Manilla in the nineteenth century. Richard never married but John had four children, three boys and a girl. The boys, one of whom, William, practised as a doctor in Manilla until he died in 1949, and another, John, who taught physics at Cambridge, left no heirs. Mary, however, married a Frenchman in the wine business, and her daughter married Monsieur Miailhe. They were the parents of Alain and May Elianne.

The family tree in Alain Miailhe's office shows his descent from many of the aristocratic families of Ireland and England and he races through it knowledgeably:

> The Clanrickards, de Burgos, died out. The last one, who was a cousin on my mother's side, was Sir William Teeling. He used to come and visit us quite regularly. His mother was a Burke. I am also related to the Lynchs – my paternal great-grandmother was a Bourran, and that was the closest family the Lynchs had left. We are related to the Lynchs a hundred times over on both sides. I am also related to the Mitchells who had the glass works and after whom Place Mitchell in Bordeaux is named. In Bordeaux there are the Kirwans, Lynchs and the Mitchells on one side and the Bartons, Lawtons and Johnstons on the other. Both were Irish but one was Anglo-Irish.

His grandmother's family, the Burkes, did well in the Philippines. They were lawyers and doctors, and some property and a chair at the university still exist. Today M. Miailhe is one of the best-known figures in the Médoc, and apart from making the excellent Château Siran wine he is involved in academic work and in the artistic world. Each year he chooses a different modern artist to design the label for his bottles.

Both M. Miailhe and his sister, Madame de Lencquesaing, who are estranged from each other following a family dispute over the division of the inheritance when their father died, speak of Comte Lynch:

> Lynch was right to hand over the keys of the city to Beresford and the Duc d'Angoulême. Bordeaux was starving [says M. Miailhe].

He was proved right by what happened at Toulouse. The Battle of Toulouse was useless because Napoleon had already left Paris. Lynch saved Bordeaux from a useless fight.

Madame de Lencquesaing is less complimentary:

He is not a cousin we are very proud of. When the king came back he changed sides. That is very typical of Bordeaux. It is a city of merchants and they did not mind political ideals as long as business went on as well; if it was a king it was all right; if it was England it was all right; if it was the Revolution it was all right. It is not very noble in a way.

Her father bought Château Pichon-Longueville, Comtesse de Lalande, in 1925 and ran it until his death in 1959. A period of co-ownership with her brother and sister ended twenty years later when lots were drawn from a basket to divide the inheritance:

I got Pichon. My elder sister got shares in Château Palmer and L'Ile Margaux and real estate in Paris. My brother got Château Siran, forest in Lalande and real estate in Paris. Pichon had been only a summer house but I came and lived here because I believe you have to live in the château to run the estate properly.

Château Pichon-Lalande is sumptuous. When her father bought it from the Pichon-Longueville family it came complete with its 1840 furniture, including the traditional black pieces which royalist families always kept in one room as a sign of mourning for the monarchy. She restored the house fully and is engaged in sorting through archives going back decades, which were removed to the attic when the house was occupied by the Germans during the last war.

The château was designed by Duphot and built about 1840. It is a copy of a much earlier Lalande town-house in Bordeaux which, when its owners, the parents of Comte Henri de Lalande who married into the Pichon-Longueville family, were guillotined, had been turned into a prison.

Madame de Lencquesaing and her husband General Hervé de Lencquesaing, who served in Morocco, Normandy and Alsace during the last war and later in

Indo-China, run the estate together. There are several paintings in the château by Sophie de Pichon-Longueville, sister of the Comtessse de Lalande, who had studied under the painter Gerard in Paris. They include a curious depiction of the Irish legend of Oisin.

Across the road in Pauillac is Château Pichon-Longueville, Baron, which was the property of the comtesse's brother. The vineyards are still in production but the château has been empty for many years.

There are other descendants of the Lynchs in the region. Thirty kilometres up the valley of the Gironde and some sixty kilometres south of Bordeaux, you turn sharp right off a twisting country road and are confronted by a spectacular long narrow château. It is sand-coloured with red shutters; there is a central bell tower and a gravel driveway around a lawn. You can see through the house, through the large windows, past the chandeliers and the grand piano, the cello and the portraits, to the trees and the meadows at the back.

The part of the hall which is not panelled is decorated with wallpaper of *fleur-de-lis*. The walls are adorned with engravings of former monarchs of France. In the library, at the top of the long and steep stone spiral staircase so typical of French châteaux, there are, behind the dark shutters which block the magnificent view, numerous books on history and genealogy. Handwritten family trees of the various ancestors of the present owner hang on the walls. The nobility of several countries, notably England and France but also Ireland and Italy, are represented. Valois and Bourbon kings look down from the arched ceiling.

It is undoubtedly a royalist house and one would imagine that it had been in the present family for generations. Not so. Château Lyde, built in 1632 during the reign of Louis XIII, was bought relatively recently by the Garaud family. It is now the property of Olivier Garaud (born 1950), his wife and their children. His brother, Xavier, lives in one wing. Their parents have a nearby château.

Olivier Garaud is a direct descendant, through the female line, of Jean Jacques Lynch (1712-42), uncle of Comte Lynch, and of his wife Mary French of Galway. As well as the Lynch family tree hanging in the library, M. Garaud's mother, his Lynch connection, has compiled an album of her descent. It shows her ancestor to be Henry Gratien Lynch, great-grandson of Jean Jacques. There is a photograph of Henry Gratien's daughter, Marie Alice, Berthe Lynch and of her town-house, Hôtel Lynch at 2 rue Ulysée Gayon, Bordeaux, where she and her husband, Louis Tampier, lived at the end of the last century. The Lynch arms are above the door. Their daughter Jeanne married Philippe de Fornel; their daughter Marie Marguerite married Louis Favre de Lapaillerie, and their daughter Eliane married Michel Garaud.

The album, handwritten and containing newspaper and magazine articles, has pictures of Lynch landmarks in Galway and former Lynch properties in Bordeaux, including the well-known wine châteaux. While Château Lyde is older and far less grand, both in construction and in decoration, than the magnificent châteaux in the Médoc, it is full of interest for the researcher. As well as numerous books and papers there is a fine portrait of Comte Lynch on the chimney-piece. It is a connection of which the Garauds are proud.

29: DE LA BROSSE

28: THE BEDROOM OF CARDINAL RICHELIEU, ST-GÉRY

SEVEN

AQUITAINE

The O'Byrnes and the MacCarthys

I N ONE ROOM of an immense and imposing château, part medieval and part seventeenth century, sited on a hot plain near Toulouse in south-west France, hangs eighteenth-century portraits of three Irish families. All of them had connections with the château and one, the O'Byrnes, still live there. The others are MacCarthys and O'Kelly-Farrells. Ancestors of the three families came to France during the eighteenth century, intermarried and have descendants of their name, and others, spread around the country.

The Château de St-Géry is west of Rabestens on the road to Albi some forty kilometres north of Toulouse. Although open to the public, it is off the main tourist route and is not a busy place. Hidden from the road by trees, an approach is made through a grand gate into an imposing gravelled courtyard. The château surrounds the visitor. At the back,

28   DE LA BROSSE *The 1830s château was symmetrical, with three floors, seven bays and circular corner towers at each end of the garden front. Acquired by MacCarthys at turn of the century, they added two bays to the entry front, accommodating a Louis-XVI style drawing-room large enough for their family portraits. Set in an English park with an artificial lake framed by what is said to the earliest Wellingtonia in France.*

29   ST-GÉRY *One of the finest châteaux in south-western France. Incorporates a medieval fortress concealed behind wing of a 17th-century courtyard bound on three sides by red-brick façades and approached between reclining sphinxes. Interiors reflect history of French decoration up to time of Charles X, bedrooms being remodelled to receive kings who never came.*

on the river, a large part of a once-magnificent balustrade has fallen into the Tarn and an unsightly wire fence has been erected to prevent mishaps. The collapse occurred in the early 1970s and, as with so much else in this unique château, Monsieur and Madame O'Byrne have no money to repair it.

M. O'Byrne, born in 1904, is the great-grandson of the Edward O'Byrne who married into the family of the Marquis de St-Géry in 1827, but the family's Irish links began when the 1st Marquis de St-Géry, Clement de Rey, a member of the parliament of Toulouse, married Marie O'Kelly-Farrell in 1767. He was guillotined during the Revolution. The last marquis married Marie Christine de MacCarthy Reagh of the family of Justin MacCarthy Reagh of Toulouse.

Mademoiselle MacCarthy Reagh and the Marquis de St-Géry had eight daughters, according to family papers, and the youngest, Gertrude, married Edward O'Byrne, a son of John O'Byrne of Mullinahack, Co. Dublin. The O'Byrnes, of course, were chieftains of Wicklow and were among the last to hold out against English rule in Leinster, where they defeated Essex as late as 1599, but there is no evidence today of where Mullinahack actually was.*

Edward had been involved in business in Bordeaux where O'Byrnes, probably relatives, were well established in the wine trade and from where a branch of the family fled back to Ireland during the Revolution. For a time Edward served in the French army but on his marriage he took over the St-Géry château and estate.

The couple had four children. Their eldest son, John, married Eleanore de Hubner, daughter of Austrian diplomat Count Joseph Hubner, went to Ireland and settled at

---

* There was a Mullinahack in Dublin city in the eighteenth century, however, and an area between Cooke Street and Bridgefoot Street is still known by this name. Mullinahack means dirty mill and Dirty Lane, now Upper Bridgefoot Street, got its name from just such a mill.

Corville near Roscrea. Their daughter Mary O'Byrne married John A. O'Kelly, grandfather of the present Count Eoin O'Kelly of Gallagh. Edward and Gertrude's third son, Henry, stayed at St-Géry, and his grandson is the present owner.

M. O'Byrne is slightly frail and his Parisian wife, Marie de Deckar, appears to take charge. They are immensely welcoming but hire a guide to take visitors on the daily tour of the château. It is obvious they love their house and are aware of its uniqueness, untouched for hundreds of years, and they are proud, in an unpretentious way, to show it off. They have no title. They could, said M. O'Byrne, claim the designation Marquis de St-Géry, since they own the house and are direct descendants of the last marquis, but they have not got the resources to do so. In any case, he says, he is unconcerned with these matters and gives the impression of disapproval of such affectations, so common in republican France today.

Neither Monsieur nor Madame speak more than a few words of English but they are aware of their Irish background and proud of it. They have been to Ireland and know their nearest relatives there, Count O'Kelly and his family.

In the small ground-floor library of the wing where they live they produce faded and tattered bits of paper showing their ancestry. A picture of Marie Christine MacCarthy Reagh hangs on the wall. She is holding a baby and it is more homely than the same La MacCarthy, as the family call her, in the grand drawing-room upstairs. An old map of Dublin is also on display.

Photographs of the couple's nine children and numerous grandchildren adorn the room. One son, Gerald, an architect, lives at St-Géry. They are a very Catholic family. M. O'Byrne had an aunt a nun, a brother is a missionary priest with the White Fathers, and two of his sisters are also nuns.

One, Monique, was a nurse with the Red Cross and won the Croix de Guerre for her work in the last war. His father was awarded a Croix de Guerre in the First World War.

The tour of the château begins in the kitchen, which dates from the fourteenth and fifteenth centuries. It has a stone floor, huge range and high windows. It was built by the la Roque Boullacs, who sold St-Géry to Monsieur de Rey in 1728. Elsewhere on the ground floor is a tiny fourteenth-century chapel with frescos of the marriage of Mademoiselle de la Roque Boullac. In the second, eighteenth-century chapel M. O'Byrne's brother, Fr Gerald, says Mass on special occasions.

Off the long gallery upstairs the bedrooms have been decorated to mark different periods. The grandest of them, where shuttered windows are opened to reveal the river Tarn far below, once accommodated Cardinal Richelieu for two nights. The big four-poster bed is hung with pink drapes and covered with a similar bedspread. It is surrounded by railings and all the furniture is Louis XIII. A magnificent tapestry of Lot and his daughters, with his wife being turned into salt, hangs on the wall and there is much wood panelling.

A copy of a letter from Richelieu to M. de la Roque Boullac is on display in a glass case. It is dated August 1629 and states, "I am sending you an order to receive and guard the hostages of Montauban."

The yellow bedroom is Louis XV, the blue room Louis XVI and the green room Empire period. In the six-metre-high rococo salon are engravings of the Walsh and Berwick regiments of the Irish Brigades.

In another grand salon hang portraits of the parents of La MacCarthy, of the brother of the 1st Marquise de St-Géry, Monsieur O'Kelly-Farrell (who, the O'Byrnes tell us, was an Ambassador of France in the mid-eighteenth century), and of the Bourbon monarchs and their families.

Of all the Wild Geese families, the MacCarthys appear to have been the most numerous, yet there are surprisingly few to be found now. Originally based in the Bordeaux-Toulouse area, the chief representatives of this old Irish family, dozens of whom came to France, are the elderly Mesdemoiselles Gabrielle and Eglé MacCarthy, and their sister Kathleen, widow of General Roger d'Hautville, who live at Château de la Brosse, near Laurent-en-Gâtines in north-central France. There is also Colonel Marcel Dugue MacCarthy of Paris, whose father added his mother's name of MacCarthy to his father's Dugue, and who is a cousin of the three MacCarthy sisters.

These French MacCarthys are descended from a nephew of Denis MacCarthy, a member of a senior branch of the Clan Diarmud house of the MacCarthy Reagh of Carbery, Co. Cork, who moved to France after the fall of Limerick in 1691 and the loss of his estates. He settled in Bordeaux, founded a trading house and wine château, bought an estate in Graves and was one of the city's leading citizens at a time when there were many Irishmen in business there.

Denis MacCarthy became director of the Chamber of Commerce in 1767 and its first consul the following year. He was admitted to the ranks of the French nobility in 1756 and became 'seigneur de Beauje, Fondival et Marliere', having proved his nobility by descent from the MacCarthy Reagh and his relationship to the Duke of Clancarthy. A genealogical map, dated 1913, showing the family's descent from Rameau (a branch) de Clan Diarmud, is in Château de la Brosse today.

Denis and his wife Jane Fitzgerald had no heirs, and he invited his two nephews, Daniel and John MacCarthy, who were living with their father, Thomas, in Co. Tipperary, to come to Bordeaux. They were educated at the College of Vendôme and later became French citizens. The business, which lasted until 1828, was now called 'MacCarthy Frères', and as well as Château MacCarthy in the Médoc, which still trades, the family owned the Hôtel MacCarthy, their splendid town-house which stands at 25 Cours de Verdun in Bordeaux. The MacCarthys were among the richest wine merchants in the city.

Daniel married Eleanore, daughter of Comte Sutton de Clonard of Wexford, an officer in the Irish Brigades who had been prominent in the East Indies Company. (Her sister, Frances, married the Marquis Jean de Bugeaud and was the mother of Napoleon's Marshal Bugeaud, later Duc d'Isly.) Daniel's brother John married Cecile O'Byrne, whose family, originally from Cabinteely, Co. Dublin, owned Château de la Houringue (see Chapter Five).

The two brothers were admitted into the ranks of the French nobility at Fontainebleau in 1785 and, with their uncle, were members of the Estates-General of 1789. During the 1793 Terror Daniel was imprisoned, with hundreds of others, as a suspect and he died soon afterwards. Meanwhile his brother John left Bordeaux for Hamburg and did not return till this turbulent period was over. John had a son, Denis Edward, who became a judge of the Tribunal of Commerce and a regent of the bank, and who in turn left two daughters.

Daniel's eldest son, John, married Françoise Georgina Lawton, of another distinguished Irish wine-trading family, and they had three children. He was a successful business-man and travelled frequently to England, Scandinavia, Scotland and Ireland. As a keen royalist he had to retreat to England during the 100 Days of Napoleon's return from Elba, but he came back to Bordeaux after Waterloo.

John and Françoise's son, Daniel Robert, born in 1826, married Hélène de Pichon and they had one son, Patrice, born in 1874. Patrice married Viva Exshaw, of yet another Bordeaux Irish family, and their three daughters live today at Château de la Brosse, while their one son, Donald, Comte MacCarthy, died young and without heirs in 1925.

Daniel Robert's sister married M. Dugue, and their son added the name MacCarthy to his own. Colonel Marcel Dugue MacCarthy, their grandson, is a military historian. He had several brothers, but they were killed in the last war and in Vietnam. He has one daughter.

Madame d'Hauteville, who is eighty-five with four grown-up children, spent much of her life in Morocco where her late husband was in the army. She speaks with knowledge of her ancestors. Her father, Patrice, moved from Bordeaux and bought Château de la Brosse with the money his wife, Viva Exshaw, brought to the marriage.

> The Exshaws were very wealthy. They had been publishers in Dublin originally and my mother spoke English. My brother died of polio at nearly twenty-five years so when my sisters die the direct MacCarthy line is gone.

According to documents at La Brosse, the Clan Diarmud MacCarthy Reagh at La Rochelle, at Grenoble and at Toulouse all died out without male heirs and the title comte went to Daniel Robert and then to Madame d'Hauteville's father, Patrice, and brother, Donald.

Henri d'Hauteville, Kathleen d'Hauteville's son, says he believes his two aunts may be the last of all the MacCarthys that came to France who still bear the name:

> There has been just one son and many daughters over the generations and there are only three old women living at La Brosse now. What will happen when they die? There are four of us and we live in different areas of France. It is very difficult to have three or four owners of the same house.

The parklands of La Brosse, which were specially designed in the English style and contain rare conifers brought from England, are less well kept than they used to be. The surrounding estate land of 350 hectares is let to local farmers.

In his *Biographical Dictionary of Irishmen in France* (Dublin 1949) Richard Hayes lists ten MacCarthys, all from Munster, representatives of old Gaelic Ireland who emigrated to France independently on the confiscation of their family estates between the Flight of the Earls in 1607 and the Treaty of Limerick in 1691.

The most prominent were the MacCarthys of Muskerry. Donough MacCarthy, son of Sir Charles MacCarthy, Viscount Muskerry, left Ireland after the breakup of the Confederation of Kilkenny, of which he and his brother-in-law, the Earl of Ormond (see Chapter Eight), were leading members, and the confiscations that followed the rebellion of 1641. MacCarthy Muskerry, later created Earl of Clancarthy, went with 5000 retainers to join Charles II on the Continent and settled in Paris.

His younger son, Justin MacCarthy, Lord Mountcashel, left Ireland in 1690 and landed at Brest with 5800 Irish soldiers to form the Irish regiment which Louis XVI demanded in exchange for those sent to Ireland under Lauzun. He saw service in France, Spain, Italy and Germany but died in 1694 of a wound received in an earlier campaign in France. He left no heirs but passed his titles to his cousin Florence MacCarthy of the Carrignavar branch, who became 2nd Duke of Clancarthy. His son, the 3rd Duke, Callaghan MacCarthy, was killed at Fontenoy. This branch was represented in France by the 7th Duc de Clancarthy Blarney, Pol MacCarthy, who lived in Rennes until his death in the 1940s.

One of the descendants of the elder son of the 1st Earl of Clancarthy, the 5th Earl, Robert MacCarthy, joined the English navy but, failing to regain the family estates, became a keen supporter of Prince Charles Edward and was well known at the French court. He lived for many years at his château at Boulogne and was the last of his line. He died in 1770.

The descendants of Comte Justin MacCarthy, born in Co. Tipperary in 1744, who settled in Toulouse around

1776, became extinct in the male line with the death of Comte Nicholas MacCarthy in 1906. He was the son of Denis MacCarthy, head of the MacCarthy Reagh family, who had emigrated to France following the introduction of the penal laws and died at Argenton in Berri in 1761. La MacCarthy of St Géry was a member of this family.

Justin MacCarthy was a distinguished scholar and had one of the best libraries in Europe; its first editions and fine bindings, were said to rival the king's collection in Paris. On his death in 1812 Napoleon forbade its export from France despite its sale to the Duke of Devonshire. His son, Comte Robert Joseph, was an army officer who left France to join the emigrés on the outbreak of Revolution but returned after the Restoration and was appointed maréchal de camp of cavalry.

Members of Justin MacCarthy's family are often known as MacCarthy Levignac after a property he bought in Bordeaux, and his second son, the Jesuit Abbé Nicholas MacCarthy Levignac, was famed throughout France as a preacher.

Other French MacCarthys listed by Hayes include Colonel Charles MacCarthy Reagh, a noted soldier for France at the great battles of the mid-eighteenth century; Florence MacCarthy Reagh, a naval officer who became a major-general of marine and who eventually emigrated to New Orleans where his father, Callaghan MacCarthy, died in 1746 of wounds received at sea; Timothy MacCarthy Reagh, whose whole family followed him into the naval service and whose grandson received the title of vicomte in the 1770s; Sir Charles MacCarthy Lyragh, an officer in Berwick's regiment, who died fighting the Ashantis in Sierra Leone in 1824; Eugene MacCarthy, whose mother was an aunt of Daniel O'Connell and who in 1777 went with the French expeditionary force to fight in the American War of Independence and later, joining the Irish/English brigade, was among those who died of fever in the West Indies in 1801.

Still others listed include John MacCarthy of Nantes who fought with Napoleon, was decorated after Waterloo and became a publisher and one of the founders of the Geographical Society of France; his son Oscar MacCarthy, born in 1815, who settled in Algeria and planned the railway system; and Jean-Baptiste MacCarthy, a one-time priest of Nantes, executed for brigandage in 1802.

30: Kermaria

31: Le Lude

EIGHT

CENTRAL FRANCE

The Butlers and the d'Arcys

I N FRANCE the sons take the title held by their father, so there is a proliferation of comtes and vicomtes. All but the eldest son, however, use their Christian names and the head of the family is distinguished by the absence of one. The Butlers have dozens of minor nobles spread around France. They are a large family and while several Butlers emigrated during the seventeenth century, the two branches prominent in France today, comtes and vicomtes, are descended from two grandsons of a Galwayman who came to the Atlantic port of La Rochelle in 1665.

Of all Irish families in France, probably more research has been done on the Butlers than on any other. The family in Ireland, a loose assocation of those bearing the name, produces a journal which has worldwide distribution and gives details of the activities of anyone called Butler, as well as up-to-date reports on research into family genealogies and the continual quest for heirs to the several titles acquired

---

30   KERMARIA *Built at turn of the century by Jean Raymond de Butler who wanted it in Brittany, but whose wife insisted on living beside her parents in south-western France. Breton in style and name, it avoids vulgarity through being austere.*

31   LE LUDE *One of the great châteaux of the Loire celebrated for* son et lumière *spectacles that recount its past. A medieval fortress of the Nerras, Beaumonts, Briennes and Vendômes, and later transformed into a country seat during the Renaissance, firstly by the de Daillons and lastly by Françoise Butler, Marquise de Vieuville, just before the Revolution. Her architect, Gabriel Barré, built a new central range in the uncompromising classicism of Louis* XVI. *Reception rooms opening directly to the garden have been retained unaltered by her descendants.*

since the family settled in Ireland in the twelfth century. There are also annual Butler rallies held in various parts of the world, similar to the Gaelic clan rallies, although of course the Butlers were originally Norman.

Lord Dunboyne, the 28th Baron, a Butler, has been an assiduous family historian. The Butlers, he wrote, bred like rabbits once they came to Ireland, and this is part of the problem in now tracing lineage. The family arrived in England with the Normans and moved to Ireland with Henry II a century later in the 1170s. By 1185 Theobald Walter was chief butler and they took their name from the office.

The Butlers established themselves in the midlands. Edmund Butler was given the title Earl of Carrick in the fourteenth century and his brother Thomas was made Lord Dunboyne. Edmund's son James was created 1st Earl of Ormond in 1328 and married the niece of Edward III, Eleanor de Bohun. With some exceptions the family were stern upholders of English rule in Ireland and produced, among others, Anne Boleyn, mother of Elizabeth 1st; Red Piers Butler; Black Tom; the dukes of Ormond; the earls of Ossory and a lord lieutenant. They built numerous grand houses as well as Kilkenny Castle.

The first two dukes of Ormond, however, were Jacobites, at least for some period of their lives. The 2nd Duke moved from having been among King William's life-guards at the battle of the Boyne, to being attainted by George I, to joining the Old Pretender (Jacques III) at St Germain. In 1718 he was sent to Moscow to arrange a marriage between the Pretender and a daughter of Peter the Great. The mission failed but the duke's companion, Chevalier Charles Wogan of Rathcoffey, Co. Kildare, found another and very acceptable bride in the person of Princess Clementina Sobieski, granddaughter of a former king of Poland, whom he and three fellow officers from Dillon's regiment rescued from detention in the castle of Innsbruck.

The John Butler who settled in La Rochelle in the mid-seventeenth century, however, was born in Galway to John Butler and his wife Jean Bodkin, daughter of a mayor of the city. Lord Dunboyne, writing in the December 1969 issue of the *Journal of the Butler Society*, finds the origin of the Galway Butlers difficult to trace. One theory has it that they are descended from the 8th or 9th Earls of Ormond but he believes they issued from the main Butler branch earlier, possibly from Thomas, younger brother of the 1st Earl, who died in 1338. In his history of the family he says they could be descended from one of the four sons of Piers Butler of Abbeyleix.

John Butler left Galway about 1655, following the death of his father in the wars against Cromwell. He married his cousin, Marguerite Butler, whose family were already settled in La Rochelle, and with his relatives started a ship-building business. According to a descendant, Louis Pauchet, who now lives near Versailles, the Butlers possessed one tenth of the fleet of La Rochelle which was commissioned for the Americas in 1780, and acted as privateers, corsairs and traders.

By this time the family had been naturalized French and Jean and Marguerite's eldest son, Jean Baptiste, became magistrate, mayor, director of the chamber of commerce and colonel of the militia in the port. Two other sons, Richard and Robert, bought properties in the French Caribbean colony of Saint-Domingue and it is from Richard (1690-1722) that the French de Butlers are descended, one of his sons becoming Comte de Butler and the other Vicomte de Butler.

At the end of the eighteenth century the Butlers and many other French noble families had extensive and rich plantations in Saint-Domingue and spent much of their time commuting between France and the West Indies. The Butlers improved their position by advantageous marriages which added to their fortune and social status and, like many other Irish families, they had the French genealogist Pierre d'Hozier draw up a pedigree of noble birth. The application, which was recognized by the French authorities in 1779, speaks of John Butler of Galway having taken up arms against "the perfidious rebel Cromwell, usurper of the Kingdom of England, Scotland and Ireland" and of battling with courage until he lost his life.

The Revolution, however, which spread to the colonies and temporarily freed the slaves on which the economy was based, brought all this prosperity to an end. While the mainland French nobility, at least those who survived, recovered much with the Restoration, the fabulous wealth of the colonies and of families like the Butlers, whose maritime business depended on them, was gone for ever. The unfortunate Toussaint l'Ouverture, who was made commander-in-chief of the island by the Convention in 1797 and later died in a dungeon in France, had been a slave on one of the Butler plantations near what is now Cap Haiti.

One of the Caribbean Butler heiresses, however, married François, Marquis de Vieuville, and inherited the Château du Lude on the Loire from her uncle M. de Velaer. She commissioned Barré to build a Louis-xvi wing facing the garden with the Butler coat-of-arms in the pediment (a feature first mentioned by Canon Dunlop of Salisbury Cathedral in his Loire guide-book published in the 1970s). The family held the château throughout the Revolution and today it is owned by her descendants.

The vicomte's or junior branch of the family lost everything in the Revolution because they had few business interests in France, but the senior line continued to be rich and influential. The Comte de Butler, Jean Pantaleon (1753-1815), who lived in the most turbulent times, was related to much of the old nobility of France through both his mother, Julie d'Hericourt, and his wife, the heiress Marie

Antoinette Reine de Jassaud, who was guillotined during the Terror of 1794.

Jean Pantaleon spent the enormous sum of £18,000 on having the Chevalier O'Gorman, the Clare-born specialist in Irish genealogy, friend to Louis xv and Burgundy estate-owner through his wife's family, the d'Eons, establish his noble background so he could be presented to the king and admitted to the honours of court. However, court and king were swept away before he got the chance to achieve his ambition and he spent the rest of his life at the centre of numerous royalist intrigues, attempting to save the king from the guillotine and later restoring the Bourbons.

Acting as what would be called today a trouble-shooter for the exiled princes, Jean Pantaleon was attached to the court in exile of the Duc d'Artois, later Charles x, and lived in Germany, London and Madrid, from which countries he undertook dangerous missions on behalf of the royalists into republican France. He died in Sweden.

His son Charles Jean Edouard, 4th Comte de Butler, was an officer in the army of Louis xviii and he acquired the Château de Remaisnil in Picardy, which remained in the family for about 100 years before it was bought by the late fashion tycoon, Laura Ashley. Originally built by the Montmorency family, it came to the Butlers through marriage.

The 6th Comte, who married a lady-in-waiting to the Queen of Portugal, received from the queen's husband, King Carlos, the concession to all exploration in Portuguese Guinea, West Africa, for a period of ninety-nine years. Although consequently a landlord of eight million acres, he did not make his fortune and, according to Louis Pauchet, only a magnificent gold watch, a gift from Queen Amelie, remains in the family from this adventure.

The 7th Comte de Butler, Raymond, born in 1889, was a professor of medicine in Amiens. His son, Tanguy, lives at the Château de Noeux-les-Auxi near Calais, a twelfth-century castle which came to the family through marriage and has never been sold.

Jacques, Vicomte de Butler, head of the junior branch, lives in the Château dè Kermaria at the south-west tip of the Massif Central. He is a retired army officer who served for twenty-five years in the French administration in Morocco but on its independence returned to France and became an inspector-general of the economy in the ministry of economics and finance. He has six brothers and six sisters, numerous nieces and nephews and a dozen grandchildren.

The vicomte has a great amount of genealogical material but regrets that so much documentation relating to the family was lost in Saint-Domingue where the title of nobility was registered in 1770. His branch of the family also lived in La Rochelle during this period where they had both a town-house and châteaux – Gouzangre and La Crapaudière – in the country, but their wealth came from trading between France and the Caribbean, and from their colonial estates.

> When we returned to France after 1790 we were ruined. We had all our fortune in Saint-Domingue and my ancestor even had to sell his house in La Rochelle. All that rests are the accounts. They show that we were proprietors and had slaves but we were never in the slave trade. We were in sugar and coffee.

An account book at Kermaria shows that in 1776 one Butler plantation had 189 slaves and 88 mulattos, as well as 10 horses and several other animals.

The vicomte is descended from Pierre Antoine, Richard de Butler's second son, who had married Elizabeth Bodkin de Fitzgerald, and today there are thirty Butler vicomtes of roughly the same age. A grandson of Pierre Antoine, Jean Raymond de Butler, joined the French army and became a general. He built Kermaria because his wife came from this area near Villefranche. The present Vicomte de Butler, who was born in 1912, is his grandson.

The family tree which hangs in the library at Kermaria starts in the fifteenth century with the marriage of Thomas de Butler and Marie de Burgo, and shows Butler marriages to O'Connors, Lynchs and O'Malleys. The small château is in remote country and surrounded by woods. There are many family portraits and the Butler arms are portrayed in a stained-glass window on the wooden staircase.

Another family with a similar background is the d'Arcys, who were also Jacobites and left Galway only a few decades later than the Butlers. They too were Normans who had come to England with William the Conqueror, moved to Ireland and then returned to France in the seventeenth century.

Count Sam d'Arcy, brother of the present Comte d'Arcy, lives in Kent in England and has done considerable research into the family background. His cousin Baron d'Arcy, Richard Emmanuel, lives outside Paris and many of the family papers are in the Paris home of his step-mother Baronne Manuela d'Arcy, daughter of one of the founding families of Genoa, the Marquis Serra.

The d'Arcys were originally seigneurs in Normandy who were granted land in Lincolnshire by William the Conqueror. Thomas, the 1st Baron, fought in France with Henry II's son, Richard Coeur de Lion, and the 4th Baron, James, who married Jane de Burgh, founded the two main branches of the family, the peers of England who died out in 1778 and those who came to Ireland. The Irish family, whose principal home was the now ruined Clifden Castle in Co. Galway, numbered among its members a viceroy and a Count of Galway. They were married into Butlers, Martyns and Dillons.

Some members of the family were engaged in the wine trade with Bordeaux and it was this branch that left Ireland after the battle of the Boyne. James d'Arcy, third son of Hyacinth of Kiltullagh, Co. Galway, where the ruined castle still remains, settled in Bordeaux during the reign of Louis xv. His brother Martin lived for a time in Brest and joined the military establishment of the Prince de Condé. He later became a banker in Paris and was so successful that he acquired properties all over the city, including three mansions in St Germain and in Faubourg du Roule and most of the quartier Beaujon. He died without children in 1769.

James's son Richard, who married Jane Kirwan, became an officer in Lally's regiment and spent four years in Martinique in command of the French troops there. With his cousin Patrick, a scientist and officer in the regiment of Fitzjames, he got letters of naturalization and recognition of nobility from Prince Charles Edward Stuart in 1758. Richard died in Paris in 1781 and is buried at St Sulpice.

Patrick, Comte d'Arcy, grandson of Hyacinth and son of John d'Arcy and Jane Lynch, daughter of Sir Robert Blosse Lynch of Castle Carra, Co. Mayo, was born in 1725 in Ireland and was widely known in France, where he arrived at the age of fourteen, as both a soldier and a scientist. He wrote several treatises on mechanics and hydraulics and after his death, the philosopher and mathematician Condorcet wrote an account of his achievements. Place d'Arcy in Dijon is probably named after him because of his work in bringing a water supply to the city.

---

32   VAL *Fairytale 15th-century château built by the d'Estaings on a rocky peak in a remote mountain valley, restored by M. Suchard during the Second Empire to house his collection of Renaissance furniture, tapestries and paintings, including an immense 'Bacchus' by Rubens. Inherited by wife of Patrice d'Arcy, the château remained intact till 1948 when it was decided to submerge it for a reservoir. Reprieved after an outcry, the level of the water was fixed just beneath its walls. Interiors were medievalized to compensate for its emptiness.*

32: VAL

Comte d'Arcy joined his uncle, Martin, in Condé's regiment and served in Flanders and Germany. At the battle of Fontenoy he was aide-de-camp to Marshal Saxe. In 1746 he was captured by the English while on his way to join Prince Charles Edward in Scotland and when released devoted himself to his studies in France. He was elected a member of the Académie de Science. At one stage he travelled to Ireland to assess the prospects for a possible French expedition and surveyed the coasts and harbours for this purpose.

Comte d'Arcy died of cholera in 1779 and was survived by his widow, his cousin, known as La Belle d'Arcy, who was a lady-in-waiting to Marie Antoinette and a fashionable hostess of the time. The title passed to his cousin Richard.

Richard d'Arcy's father had been a successful and rich man who rose to the rank of colonel in Lally's but his son who was born in 1755 and also served in Martinique, was ruined by the Revolution and got a job as a tax inspector under Napoleon. He died in 1831. The two grand hôtels, or town-houses, which the family had acquired in St Germain were lost. His son Hyacinth died aged twenty-three on the retreat from Moscow with Napoleon's army. His second son, born in 1802, became minister of the house of the king under the Restoration, and his son Auguste René Wilfred, born in 1833, left eleven children.

For five decades the d'Arcys owned the dramatic Château de Val at Bort-les-Orgues in the very centre of France, but it was not a family property. A fortified site from early times, the present castle was built in the fifteenth century and came into the hands of the d'Arcys in 1898, when the wife of Patrice, Vicomte d'Arcy, inherited it. In 1949 the family were forced to sell Val to make way for a reservoir in the valley it dominates. The contents have been dispersed. Today, owned by the town, the Château de Val stands surrounded by water with just a narrow causeway for entry. It was featured on a French stamp in 1966.

33: Chéne Vert

34: St Gervais
-la-Forêt

35: Colombiers

JDW 03

NINE

EASTERN FRANCE

de Warrens, MacCartans, de Walls,
Bonaparte Wyses

COMTE RAOUL DE WARREN is probably the most
knowledgeable on his background of all the Wild
Geese descendants in France. He is a scholar, committed
royalist and author, who early in life came to Ireland to
write his book *L'Irlande et ses Institutions Politiques*, published in 1928. His family history comprehensively traces
the progress of his ancestors from their arrival in England
in 1138 to their return, via Ireland, to France with James II
shortly after defeat at the battle of Cavan in 1690.

The Warrens were originally Normans who came to
England with William the Conquerer and were known
as les Comtes de Warren et de Surrey. Edward Warren

33   CHÊNE VERT *Built in an ilex grove by the Rhône in 1865, overlooking
Avignon on the far bank, for the Russian, Count Semenov, by a
Parisian architect who painted a striking portrait of the count's
beautiful wife. Inherited by a daughter-in-law who disappeared
during the Russian Revolution, passed on to her grandson William
Bonaparte Wyse and sold to the corporation, who resold it to M. and
Mme Simonnet.*

34   ST GERVAIS-LA-FORÊT *Built in two halves: the first in 1844 by de
la Morandière when restoring the château of Blois visible from the
garden front; doubled in size in 1873, the architect disguised his
addition to the garden by duplicating and recentering the existing
façade, and treated his addition to the entry front as if it were the
original medieval château.*

35   COLOMBIERS *Medieval, moated château flanked by towers, rebuilt in
18th century. Acquired by the de Walls in 1788, they built a new entry
pavilion to display their arms. Today the home of Comte Georges de
Wall.*

107

moved to Ireland in 1302 and settled at Corduff Castle near Castleknock in north-west Dublin. There they married into the Plunketts and the Husseys and had lands at Sillock (now the Finglas/Ballymun area) and at Seatown, which lies north of the Malahide estuary at Swords. On the arrival of Oliver Cromwell in 1649 their lands were confiscated, their castles burned and the family was exiled to Connacht.

The Warrens then returned to Leinster and settled at Bellaghmoon, Co. Kildare. Raoul de Warren's research states that this Edward Warren, the fifth in Ireland to bear the name, and his wife Anne Kennedy are buried at Castledermot, Co. Kildare. Their son, also Edward, born in 1666, fought for the Jacobite cause and emigrated to France after the surrender of Limerick in 1691. He is Raoul's ancestor.

At one stage during the Jacobite wars Edward Warren was taken prisoner, lodged in the Tower of London and condemned to death. Released as part of an exchange deal, he married Anne Speight, niece of a fellow inmate Lord Aylesbury, and in 1693 the couple settled in Lorraine. As captain of the infantry regiment of Dublin he served in the Palatinate campaign of 1696 and later, living in Nancy, became director of archery and gunpowder to the Duc de Lorraine.

Edward Warren died in 1733 and left several children. Having furnished proof of the high rank of his family in Ireland over hundreds of years, he was admitted to the nobility. A sketch of him in the costume of a cavalier, with armour, long hair and moustache, hangs in Raoul de Warren's château at Blois on the Loire.

Edward's son, also Edward, was born in London in 1697 and became head of archery to the dukedom of Lorraine as well as taking charge of the factories manufacturing gunpowder and saltpetre which his father had established. He was made Grand Duc de Tuscan and military governor of

Florence and married Marie Thérèse de Mageron. They had eight children. His son Henry, who died in 1781, left two sons who both served in the Irish Brigades – Jean, Comte de Warren, and Patrick.

Jean joined Dillon's regiment at the age of thirteen. Shortly after the outbreak of the Revolution, he, his brother and eight other Irish officers refused to take a new form of oath to the state from which the king's name was excluded. They left France and entered the Austrian army in the regiment of Stuart, commanded by their uncle, Francis Warren. They later joined the French emigré princes.

Known as the Chevalier de Warren, Jean also saw service in India, where he fought in the campaign against Tippoo Sahib, King of Mysore, and in Java. After the restoration of the Bourbons he returned to France, rejoined the army and was given the title comte. He died at Pondicherry in 1830.

Apart from his military adventures, the Chevalier Warren was something of a poet, and Richard Hayes quotes the following two verses from a poem in support of the royalists:

> *Les Irlandais, par leur vaillance,*
> *Soutiens des Stuarts, des Bourbons,*
> *Purent jadis cueillir en France*
> *Plus d'un laurier sous les Dillons*

> *Fidèles à nos maîtres,*
> *Reconnaissants de leurs bienfaits*
> *Sachons imiter nos ancêtres*
> *Amis, ne les quittons jamais.*

Jean's brother, Patrick de Warren, left the Austrian army and joined, with other members of the Irish Brigades, the force that some Irish officers attempted to raise in Ireland to fight under the English flag for the Bourbon Restoration. They were partially successful, but the regiment was dispatched by the British to the West Indies instead of being sent to France and, along with many others, Patrick did not return. He died of yellow fever in Jamaica in 1796.

Another member of the family was Richard Warren, a cousin, who was born at Corduff Castle in 1705. He first set up as a trader in Marseilles but then joined his two brothers in the Irish Brigades, serving in Lally's and later in Rothe's. He went to Scotland with Prince Charles Edward in 1745 and the following year was sent to the French court at Versailles to seek reinforcements for the Stuart cause from Louis xv. Before this expedition, which historians believe was to be led by another Irishman, Anthony Walsh (see Chapter Three), could be prepared, Bonny Prince Charlie had been defeated at Culloden.

It was Warren, however, who, with Captain Sheridan, and after several other efforts had failed, chartered the heavily gunned privateers *Heureux* and *Prince Conti* at St Malo, and sailed to Scotland in August 1747, rescued the Prince at Loch nan Uamh and brought him back to France.

Richard Warren was conferred with the title of baron by the Old Pretender, or 'Jacques Trois' as Raoul de Warren calls him, and was made a colonel and a knight of Saint Louis by the French king for his services to the Stuarts. He died in 1775.

Raoul de Warren and the main branch of the family are descended from Jean and his son, Edward. Born at Madras in 1811, Edward was educated at the military academy of Saint Cyr, emigrated to India and served in many wars. In 1864, in an unusual move for the period, he and his family came to Ireland for several months to renew family ties.

Edward's son, Lucien, in turn had two sons: Edward, who for many years at the beginning of this century was parliamentary deputy for Nancy, and William, Raoul's father, who was killed in the First World War.

Raoul de Warren was born in 1905 and today lives in the house his wife inherited, Château de St Gervais-la-Forêt, on a hill overlooking Blois and the river Loire. His brother Marc lives at Château de Fontaine outside Paris. St Gervais, which has a wonderfully lived-in air despite the old family portraits and the magnificent furniture, has been in the late comtesse's family, the Montrichards, since before the Revolution.

The Comte de Warren is a doctor of law and has a diploma in political science. His book on Ireland's political institutions gained him membership of the Institut de France but his main work has been as a genealogist and he has written several studies on the Pretenders to the French throne. He unequivocally believes that the Duc d'Anjou has the greatest claim but does not subscribe to any of the organizations plotting his return. His book, *La Maison de Warren* 1138-1964, was published privately.

North-east of the de Warren's old home of Nancy, alongside the border with Belgium, is the city of Lille. In the early nineteenth century, Marie Angélique MacCartan, maternal grandmother of the late President Charles de Gaulle of France, lived here. Research which General de Gaulle and his brother, Pierre, Mayor of Paris, instigated in the 1940s indicated that Marie Angélique was descended from Anthony MacCartan of Co. Down, who in 1710 at the age of sixteen joined his uncle, Lieutenant-Colonel Magennis, in Galmoy's regiment of the Irish Brigades. By 1735 Anthony was a captain in Berwick's and married to Suzanne de Coetlogon, who was Irish on her mother's side. Later research, however, which was published during the general's visit to Ireland in May 1969, stated that his great-grandmother was in fact Josephine MacCartan, the granddaughter of Dr Andronicus MacCartan, who emigrated from Co. Down to Lille in the early part of the eighteenth century.

The MacCartans, whose original name was given as

MacArtan, were chieftains in the area of Dundrum, Co. Down, and the ruins of the chapel built as a family memorial by Phelimy MacCartan in 1626 still remain. Members of the clan fought alongside Owen Roe O'Neill at the battle of Benburb in 1646 and after the defeat of the Stuarts and the confiscation of their lands several of them are known to have emigrated to France. General de Gaulle was certainly descended from the MacCartans of Lille, who were well known in medical circles in the city, but there does not appear to be anyone of the name still resident there.

Also in the east of France but much farther south, in the wine district of Burgundy, is the Château de Colombiers, home of the de Wall family, who were fervent Jacobites and came to France at a similar period and distinguished themselves in the Irish Brigades.

Patrick Wall was born at Myshall, Co. Carlow, in 1726 and at twenty years of age he went to Scotland to join Prince Charles Edward. Wounded at Culloden, he sailed for France with the Duke of Perth and joined first the Irish regiment of Rothe and later the cavalry corps of Fitzjames. He fought at Laufelt, Maastricht, in the Seven Years' War and at Rosbach. After the war he was given the title comte, promoted to the rank of lieutenant-general and admitted to the honours of court.

For a period during the 1780s General Comte de Wall was military governor of Paris and in 1779, when there were proposals for a French invasion of Ireland, he presented a military description of the country to the French ministry of war. On the outbreak of the Revolution he joined the emigré nobles abroad but returned after the Peace of Amiens and died in 1809.

Almost a century earlier, cousins of Patrick Wall, Oliver, Matthew and Richard Wall, left their home at Ballynakill, Co. Carlow, when Cromwell confiscated their father's estate. After defeat at Limerick all three emigrated to France and entered the army where they died on active service – Oliver at the siege of Lerida (in Spain) in 1707, Matthew at the siege of Barcelona in 1706 and Richard at the siege of Cremona in 1702.

Another group of Wall brothers, whom Richard Hayes says were the first Wild Geese to join the French army, were Michael, Richard, Edmund and Gerard, sons of Gerard Wall of Coolnamuck, Co. Waterford, who joined as officers in 1632 and brought a regiment of 3000 men from Ireland with them.

The branch at Colombiers, however, are descended from General Comte Wall. One of his sons, Marie Patrick, born in Paris in 1764, entered military service and married the niece of the Duc de Rohan. He was mysteriously murdered in 1787 in the forest of Fontainebleau and because he was so well known at court the discovery of his body created a sensation. The year previously he had resigned from a masonic lodge and there was speculation that masonic intrigues, which were rife in the Irish Brigades, and among Jacobites generally, lay at the root of the matter.

Marie Patrick's brother, Angélique Patrick, also served in the Irish Brigades but during the Revolution he emigrated and only returned with the Restoration. As commander of the Garde Royale and the other regiments in Paris he has been described, according to Hayes, as the last member of the Irish Brigades to draw a sword in defence of the elder branch of the Bourbons.

Today Georges de Wall is the representative of the family. He spends some of the year at Château de Colombiers but lives mostly in Marseilles. Colombier was bought by Angélique Patrick, also known as Ulrick de Wall, just before the Revolution but sold by order of the state when he joined the emigré nobles at Coblenz. He repurchased it on the Restoration. His son, a page to Charles x, was also an army officer. The château has been neglected for some years but attempts are now being made at restoration.

Farther south again, near Avignon, is the Villa de Chêne Vert which, through marriage, came into the hands of a family by the name of Bonaparte Wyse. Their story is an interesting one. Letitia Bonaparte, daughter of Napoleon's brother Lucien, married Thomas Wyse of Manor St John, Roanmore, Waterford, in 1821.

The Wyses had served in several continental armies but Thomas met Letitia when he visited Rome on the grand European tour. It appears that Lucien had several daughters and little money, and when the well-connected young Irishman arrived he was prevailed upon to marry Letitia. The marriage did not work.

Letitia created a great stir in Irish society where she was surprised to find herself, as a Catholic, a second-class citizen and treated as such by the viceroy and the Castle. "I am the niece of the emperor, the daughter of the Prince of Canino and the wife of Thomas Wyse," she is reported to have screamed during one of her many scenes.

Continually having rows over precedence, she soon got bored with Ireland, and with her husband, and left the country. Thomas Wyse was somewhat relieved but continual reports of her escapades, including jumping into the pond in London's St James's Park, and indiscreet liaisons, haunted him. She returned several times to Ireland in an attempt to see her two sons and on one occasion addressed a supportive mob from the window of her hotel in Waterford.

Letitia toured the Continent with a British army officer and had three children who, much to Thomas Wyse's fury, called themselves Bonaparte Wyse. Various bills they ran up were occasionally sent to him as their father. He made continual and strenuous efforts to take 'the spurious brood' to court to stop them using his name but because Napoleon

III was anxious to avoid a scandal involving his cousin, and because Wyse refused to have the writs made out in the name Bonaparte Wyse, and because Letitia was still legally his wife and the children thereby his, these efforts came to naught. The family roamed through high society on the Continent, contracting marriages, running up debts, having arguments, throwing parties and appearing in the newspapers.

Thomas Wyse, meanwhile, had been elected to the Westminster Parliament for Tipperary, only the second Catholic MP, after Daniel O'Connell, since Emancipation in 1829. He later represented Waterford. He moved to London and ended his days, still feuding with Letitia from a distance and continually instigating legal action, as British ambassador to Athens in 1862.

Of the couple's two sons, Napoleon was unbalanced and did not leave children, but William's grandson, also William, today lives in Cornwall. Chêne Vert, which was built in 1865 for the Comte de Semenov, came to the Bonaparte Wyses when his granddaughter married into the family. William's wife, Olga Rollason, is author of *The Spurious Brood* (1969), the amusing family history.

36: North Façade, Château de Sully

TEN

BURGUNDY

The MacMahons

"I F YOUR GRANDMOTHER is an Orléans you are related to everyone." So we were told about the Duc de Magenta, and so it is. Born Philippe de MacMahon in 1938, he is descended from the Bourbon kings of France and related to the present chief claimant to the French throne, the Comte de Paris. His great-great-great-grandfather was Pedro II, Emperor of Brazil. The King of Spain, Juan Carlos – "He is my age; we played in Portugal as children and I called him Juanito" – is a relative and so are half the nobility of Europe. The ex-Emperor Bokassa is a friend.

The duke, however, bears a thoroughly Irish name and of this he is proud. He has been to Ireland only for short visits but his family tree, showing descent from a Brian Boraine (Brian Boru), High King of Ireland in

---

36 SULLY *Still a medieval moated fortress despite its many transformations, and recognizable as such from the south where its six corner towers can be made out. Its origins have been suppressed by a succession of architects, the first, Nicholas Ribonnier, acting for Gaspard de Saulx-Tavanes in 1573, inserted a rectangular courtyard into the hexagon and approached through the central archway of his façade flanked by symmetrical outbuildings. Pierre de Moray called in the architect of Langres Cathedral, d'Aviler, who replaced the two northern ranges and the corner tower between them with a single range, modelled on Versailles. The pediment of the eastern front is consecrated to the arms of the MacMahons. Many interiors were formidably remodelled by Marthe, Marquise de MacMahon, who also commissioned the vast water staircase aligned with the central staircase of the 18th-century range. In Franck's staircase hall twin flights of stairs rise along the side walls to sway and join over a central archway above a statue to the first Duc de Magenta.*

1002, through O'Briens and MacMahons, hangs elaborately framed in the small dining-room of his magnificent home, the Château de Sully near Autun in Burgundy. It ends in the mid-nineteenth century but since then MacMahon has become an illustrious name in France and his recent ancestry is well known.

There are statues, boulevards and parks all over France in memory of Marshal MacMahon (1808-93), 1st Duc de Magenta, and he is buried in splendour at Les Invalides. A life-size statue, thrown out of Algeria with all the other French monuments when independence was declared, now stands rather incongruously in a meadow at the side of Sully. His descendant is uncertain where it should be placed.

The present 4th Duc de Magenta is the marshal's great-grandson. The MacMahons came to France in the early decades of the eighteenth century. Patrick MacMahon of Dooradoyle, Limerick, and his wife Margaret O'Sullivan of Beara, had three sons and all emigrated when the MacMahon lands were confiscated. According to recent research, which has been sent to the duke at Sully, the eldest, Michael, joined the Dominicans, returned to Ireland and was Bishop of Killaloe until he died in 1807. The second, Maurice, a captain in the Fitzjames regiment of the Irish Brigade, fought with Prince Charles Edward Stuart in Scotland but returned to France after the defeat at Culloden and died without issue in 1791.

The third son, the duke's direct ancestor, was Jean-Baptiste. Born in Limerick in 1715, he attended medical school in Rheims where members of his family had previously studied and, once qualified, set up practice in the old Roman town of Autun. Among his patients were the incredibly rich Jean Baptiste de Morey and his wife, who was also his cousin, Charlotte le Belin, both of whom were stricken with a fatal disease. The 79-year-old master of Sully, de Morey, died but his wife survived, and within a short period she married the Irish doctor. MacMahon was thirty-three years old and his bride was thirty-nine. Thus, despite the efforts of several de Moreys to thwart them, did Sully come to the MacMahons.

Jean Baptiste MacMahon then set out to join the French nobility. He submitted to Louis xv a genealogy from the Ulster King-at-Arms at Dublin Castle showing that his ancestors were lords of Feenish, Inish, Arovan, Ilaun McGrath, of the island Finus and of the town of Reynanagh, now the site of Shannon airport.

Having acquired the Château d'Éguilly, also through his wife, he was given the title Marquis d'Éguilly which had previously been held by her uncle. This château, now a ruin in the process of being restored, is clearly visible today at the side of the A6 autoroute east of Dijon.

Sully and the MacMahons survived the Revolution. Charlotte and Jean Baptiste's two sons, Charles Laure and Maurice, left France to fight with the royalist emigrés abroad but the old marquise, following the death of her husband, managed, despite arrest, imprisonment and, eventually, death, to avoid having the château confiscated as a result of their allegiance. The story is told of how her servants, who had been trained in her business affairs, pretended she was still alive by preserving her body in a barrel of alcohol and placing it in her bed whenever inspectors came in. She was merely ill, they said, and were believed.

The sons returned on the Restoration and the elder, Charles Laure, 2nd Marquis d'Éguilly, who had been a colonel in the French army and helped George Washington defeat the British at Newport, Rhode Island, led a merry life at Sully with balls and hunts. He never married.

The second son, Maurice, had an eventful career. A colonel in the cavalry regiment of Lauzun, he was severely wounded during rioting at Nancy in 1790 but served several campaigns with the emigré nobles before returning to Burgundy in 1803. At the first Bourbon Restoration in 1814 he was made maréchal de camp and during the 100 Days, when Napoleon returned from Elba, he tried to raise an army to oppose him. For this he was arrested but was saved by Waterloo.

Having married the daughter of the Marquis de Caraman, Maurice had seventeen children. The eldest, Charles Marie, the 3rd Marquis d'Éguilly, was renowned for hunting on every day of the year and for his lavish and stylish hospitality at Sully. The third son, and sixteenth child, became President of France and 1st Duc de Magenta.

Edme Patrice Maurice, born at Paris in 1808, entered the military academy of Saint Cyr when he was seventeen and two years later began his army career in Algeria. In 1855, by this time a general, he was transferred to the Crimea where he took the Malakoff Fort at Sebastopol from the Russians. It was here he made his famous remark, "J'y suis, J'y reste," when told that the fort was mined and that he should withdraw.

Back in Europe he won a brilliant victory over the Austrians at Magenta in 1859 and Napoleon III created him a duke and Marshal of France. The following year a deputation from Ireland, which was joined at Paris by the Young Irelander John Mitchel, presented him with a sword of honour. In 1864 MacMahon was appointed Governor-General of Algeria and while there proposed a scheme, later abandoned, for establishing an Irish colony in North Africa. Fort MacMahon in the Algerian Sahara is named after him.

Following his second period in Algeria, MacMahon was recalled to take command at the outbreak of the Franco-Prussian War. He was defeated at Worth and then at Sedan, where he was wounded and taken unconscious from the field. Two days later the Third French Republic was declared. When peace was established MacMahon was given the task of suppressing the uprising of the Paris

Commune and in 1873 the assembly, in search of stability, made him President of the Republic.

A known monarchist, MacMahon resigned in 1879 having failed to win a monarchist majority in the assembly. He retired to Montcresson, near Orléans, and died at Château-la-Forêt in 1893.

Marshal MacMahon, Duc de Magenta, married Elisabeth de la Croix de Castries (whose grandfather the Duc de Castries had married as his second wife Elizabeth Coughlan of Ardo Castle, Ardmore, Co. Waterford), and had several children. The marshal, however, was never the owner of Sully. The château stayed with the elder branch, the descendants of Charles Marie, until the widow of his grandson, the royalist activist Marthe de Vogue, Marquise de MacMahon, willed it to the marshal's heirs when she died without children in 1923.

The marshal's eldest son, General Patrice, Duc de Magenta, married Princess Marguerite d'Orléans and their son, Maurice, 3rd Duke, married Marguerite Riquet de Caraman Chimay. Maurice, who was killed in a hunting accident in 1954, joined the French air force and served in France and in Morocco. On the outbreak of war, like so many military men, he was torn between Pétain and de Gaulle but ended up as a Resistance leader in the northern part of the country.

It was his sister, the aunt of the present duke, who suffered most terribly as a result of her Resistance work. Françoise, Comtesse de Buffières de Rambuteau, her husband and two of their three sons were sent to the concentration camp at Buchenwald when Germans dressed as Polish refugees tricked the family into helping them. The comte died there but the others survived.

The duke, who is separated from his wife, lives today in the splendour of Sully, 300 kilometres south east of Paris. He realizes, he says, that he is the luckiest man in the world to have such a beautiful home but he is also aware that it is not entirely his, as French law dictates that all property must be divided equally between the direct heirs.

> The property belongs to five of us and my mother has the benefit
> of it. We will have to sell or agree with my brother and sisters. It
> is very difficult. I love this house. I am nearly married to it. Also
> I love the country.

The duke farms 300 hectares (about 800 acres) at Sully,
mostly pasture and woodland. Since he became seriously
ill some years ago he has handed over all the running of the
farm to his agent.

> But I lose money; you can't win [make] money with farming if
> you have to have people to do it. My main occupation is farming
> and looking after the house. This is a whole-time job without staff.
> There was a leak of water in the library for six months but nobody
> had seen it. You have to keep going around.

The château is not open to the public but the grounds
are. For a 5-franc entrance fee visitors can walk around the
moat and view the splendour of one of the finest châteaux
in France, with its MacMahon and de Morey crests, its wide
staircases and immense terraces projecting into the water.

The moat is too wide, the duke says, and there being only
a single narrow bridge, if anything happened the fire hoses
would not be able to reach the house. He is not keen on the
public either, "but you have to show your house; it is my
home but it is a house of France. The visitors bring in only
a very little money; it does not pay [for] the garden."

Across the bridge and through the heavy door there is an
immense rectangular gravel courtyard bordered by orange
trees in white boxes, sheltered and secluded from the world.
On the Sunday evening we arrived, the duke and his girl-
friend were lying here on sunbeds reading magazines. A
bottle of Duc de Magenta, perfectly chilled, was produced.
Dozens of windows with no faces behind them, some thirty
life-size frescos of classical figures and many sculpted friezes
stared down upon us from all sides.

The immense château was entirely empty. Only the

conversation and the buzz of the duke's cordless phone broke the silence. It was hot and sunny and luxurious. The bees who had swarmed for years in the bell tower had been removed by experts earlier in the week. The workmen repairing the roof of the tower, badly damaged in a hailstorm and paid for by the insurance, had a day off. The public were on the other side of the moat.

Unusually, the brochure on the château shows neither the interior nor the courtyard, which is one of the most magnificent in all France. Everything across the water and behind the façade is for friends and family only.

The duke's private quarters are in a corner of the ground floor. Elsewhere there are stately rooms hung with family portraits. Signed photographs of Queen Elizabeth and of the Queen Mother in the drawing-room show that the British sovereign once came for lunch and that her mother stayed for several days. The billiard table looks unused. The finest room, a ballroom on the first floor, is used rarely. "The furniture here is only two hundred years old; it is all provincial and is not worth a fortune so we have not been burgled," the duke says.

Wine is a great joy to him, although since the onset of his illness he can drink very little. While there was always some wine made at Sully, he is immensely proud of the commercial success that now produces between 50,000 and 60,000 bottles of Duc de Magenta burgundy, red and white, each year. He has five hectares of vines.

> My family had a property or vineyard but I said I must buy a better property. I was able to borrow money cheaply and vines were not so expensive. I bought it and worked at it with all my heart. I started in 1968 and I got good bottles and I sold them around the world, even to America. I was frightened in the beginning about the loan but it is finished and the money comes in and I can live on it and it pays the insurance. Then I fell ill when everything was going well.
>
> But you need to go to school to learn how to win [make] money. That is very important. I never did that. I did not work enough. If I could re-do my life I would learn how I should work. I bought the vineyard and I made a success of it and now I am afraid to do

anything else. It is very important to learn how to work. I want to learn a computer but now I cannot see well.

When he was younger the duke hunted stag in Normandy where his mother has estates and he used to shoot. The guns hang today in his study, a protection against burglars of whom all French stately home owners are terrified.

He is thrilled by the TGV (*Train Grand Vitesse*) which passes through Sully and laughs at his outrageous, and as yet unfulfilled, plan to board the train at Paris with ten friends, pull the alarm bell at Sully and hop off across the fields for lunch at his château. He is unconcerned at the fuss that would ensue and insists that the fine would be negligible when divided by ten. He is strangely unconvinced, though, that they would discover his identity.

His love of novelty and of travel came together when he was offered five invitations, with plane tickets, to the coronation of Emperor Bokassa in what is now the Central African Republic some years ago. Since he could find no last-minute travelling companions he headed off alone and loved every minute of it. He has remained friends with Bokassa and they have frequently visited each other.

On one visit to Sully, where he normally came accompanied by his thirty ministers, the duke remembers that Bokassa insisted that the young children, who were seated at a separate table, should be served before him. "He loved children. He is said to have had fifty of his own, many of them from his time serving France in Indo-China."

The duke also remembers a trip to Africa with Bokassa and his wife Catherine. Bokassa disliked the airline's food so his wife produced a casserole from the back of the plane especially for him. He tasted a chicken leg, pronounced it good, and handed it to the duke. When the plane landed at Chad the duke advised him not to alight since there was no sign of the president in the welcoming party. The duke, however, who had gone in search of a razor at the duty-free shop, found himself toasted with champagne and paraded along the red carpet in front of a band. "It was very amusing."

He wrote to Bokassa, he says, when he was exiled in France but received no reply and there is a great note of sorrow in his voice when reminded that the ex-emperor is a condemned man. "It was his country. He had to go back."

The duke has become more religious, he says, as a result of a visit to the Marian shrine at Medagorje in Yugoslavia and because of his decision to donate a medieval ruin on his land at Sully to a community of nuns. The convent is on the site of an old monastery. Gauthier de Sully, who created the demesne, was taken prisoner in Jerusalem in 1200 while on crusade. He promised God that if he escaped and got back to France he would build a monastery. This he did and the monks stayed on the site until it was confiscated during the Revolution.

> My father bought the ruins back. Several years ago a body of religious sisters came to me and said they wanted to establish a convent there. I said I will hire it to you for one franc a year but they said 'We want to be the proprietors.' My brother and my sisters wanted to sell it but I said there would be no money for us all so I gave it to them.

Les Soeurs de Bethleém were founded in 1954 and have been established at Val Saint Benôit, near Sully, since 1982. The duke considers Soeur Marie, the founder, to be a saint.

They are a contemplative order and their convent lies in a clearing in a small forest. Their beautiful singing floats over the trees from the small semi-restored stone church. The duke visits occasionally and is thrilled by the nuns' pleasure in the place, by their success in rebuilding the ruins into a habitable dwelling, and by his decision to donate the site to them.

Is the Duc de Magenta Irish?

> No, I have an Irish name but I am French. Yes, I say I am Irish but I am French also. MacMahon was President of the French Republic and he was French. When I say I am the Duc de Magenta they say to

me 'You are Italian.' When I went to America everyone said that. I went to New York for St Patrick's Day. I was on Park Avenue but only Irish people were allowed to pass. I said I am Irish. 'What is your name?' they said. 'MacMahon' I said. So they stopped the parade to let me pass.

The duke went to preparatory school in England, but he disliked all his schools and refuses to talk about them. "I don't understand why I was put there. I hated school." He also spent some time in the army. His Irish nanny, Mollie Maher, is buried at Sully. "She was part of the family. She had brought up my mother and me."

Philippe de MacMahon is proud of his ancestors. His Irish forebears, however, are too remote to arouse great interest and are certainly overshadowed by the pedigrees of the families the MacMahons married into. He speaks of his great-great-grandfather, the Prince de Joinville, who was sent by his father Louis Philippe, King of France, to Brazil to marry Francesca, the daughter of the emperor. He brought with him his mistress, a dancer, and while curious to know what became of her after his marriage, the duke is particularly fond of the story of their romance. Seeing her on a stage in Paris, the prince wrote her a note, "Come with me, when you want, for as long as you want, and for as much as you want." She replied "Now, forever and for nothing."

Several years ago he got a letter from a girl in Ireland whose mother was born a MacMahon, wondering if they could meet to discuss a possible family connection. His reply was an immediate invitation to stay at Sully. Her answer took a long time; she was just sixteen and her parents would not allow it. He still dreams that she has green eyes.

---

40 ÉGUILLY *Medieval moated château. The gatehouses, corner towers and chapel rebuilt in the 17th century. Inherited through his wife by Jean Baptiste MacMahon, abandoned by his descendants and derelict when compulsorily purchased from the Duc de Magenta for the autoroute. Since acquired by a young couple to run an art gallery and restaurant.*

37: Staircase hall: Sully

38: Marshal MacMahon

39: Duc de Magenta

40: Éguilly

JDW '81

41: Hôtel d'Estrées, rue de Grenelle

42: Collège des Lombards, rue des Carmes, the Chapel

43: Irish College, rue des Irlandais, the Chapel

ELEVEN

PARIS AND ENVIRONS

O'Neills, St Legers, Coppingers, de Plunketts

O F ALL THE WILD GEESE families in France, the O'Neills are probably the oldest. It is known that when the Great O'Neill, Hugh, the Earl of Tyrone, sailed for the Continent from Lough Swilly in 1607 with Ruairí O'Donnell, following the surrender of 1603, he spent two weeks in France and four months in Flanders before moving on to Rome. Red Hugh O'Donnell went to Spain immediately after Kinsale. This Flight of the Earls was not only made up of the leaders but also of some family and close followers.

The Great O'Neill died in Rome in 1616. The French O'Neills, most of whom now live around Paris and in Brittany, believe they are descended from one of his sons. François O'Neill, a marine engineer and ship-builder, who is the son of the head of the family in France, Henry O'Neill, is currently engaged in research to establish the

---

41 HÔTEL D'ESTRÉES, RUE DE GRENELLE, PARIS *One of the great 18th-century hôtels of Saint Germain. Built in 1713 to design of architect Robert de Cotte. Lived in by the Regent's daughter and then, during the reign of Napoleon, by Marshal Clarke, Duc de Feltre. Now the Russian Embassy in France.*

42 COLLÈGE DES LOMBARDS, RUE DES CARMES, PARIS *Only a cobbled courtyard and chapel remains of the original Italian College acquired by the Irish College in 1672 and in use for 100 years. The church was reconstructed by an unknown architect in 1738. Since 1925 it has been the Syrian Catholic Church in Paris.*

43 THE CHAPEL, THE IRISH COLLEGE, RUE DES IRLANDAIS, PARIS *Designed by Bellanger in 1775, the whole building is currently under reconstruction. Napoleon's younger brother, Jerome, studied here, as did Pope John Paul II.*

family lineage and while documentation is missing he bases his assertions mainly on three factors.

First there is the tradition in the family that not only did they come to France with the Great O'Neill in 1607 but that they are definitely related to him; secondly is the signet ring with the O'Neill crest that has been worn by generations of his family and passed down from father to son; thirdly is their relationship to the O'Neills of the former French West Indies who, until they died out in the male line in the middle of the last century, bore the title Comtes de Tyrone. The last comte, Francis Henry, was a politician in Martinique and one of his three daughters, who died in France in 1932, was the last to hold the title Vicomtesse de Tyrone.

François O'Neill realizes that the Portuguese O'Neills hold the designation 'The O'Neill' as a result of the pact entered into before a public notary in Paris in 1901 where, as described by Richard Hayes, the Martinique O'Neills agreed that the Lisbon O'Neills were the senior branch. He believes the daughters of Francis Henry, who signed the document, were unaware of what they were doing and the seriousness of their act. There are, he says, still many facial resemblances between the French and Portuguese O'Neills.

The French O'Neills' problem is their lack of documentation and, consequently, of proof of descent. François O'Neill has drawn up a family tree starting with Hugh O'Neill in 1543. There are some gaps and he is not sure where his line lies. According to this research he believes the Great O'Neill had at least four sons and possibly others, and that at least one of them was born when O'Neill was at Besançon.

We have no papers to prove that we come from the Great O'Neill but we are sure that we are coming from him, and all the people of my family take this view. We all have this ring with the crest of

O'Neill. Many came from Ireland with O'Neill in the seventeenth century and some were from his family. We know he stayed near Besançon and we have some documents that he had some children in that place, but were the children his or his relatives?*

The furthest back the French O'Neills can go is to their ancestor François, who was born in the middle of the eighteenth century at Châlons-sur-Marne.

He went to Canada with the French army and he was chief of the military police in Quebec in 1760. He fought the English and he said 'Our family are fighting the British again.' He returned to France and was installed in Brittany. He had a lot of papers proving he was connected with the O'Neills, but these were destroyed during the Revolution.

François had eighteen children and we are descended from the eldest son. They came from Bar-le-Duc and one, Claude Alexine, asked in 1772 to be registered as coming from the Great O'Neill. Another was a general who fought in the Cameroons and in Algeria. I am trying to find more. We have a letter from one son written in 1847 which says, 'We are from Ireland and we are coming from Hugues O'Neill, Comte of Tyrone, and my father fought in Quebec. My father was also surgeon-chief of the navy of France and he was jailed by the Republicans, and my mother burned all the documents of the family because she was afraid he was shown as a loyalist.'

François O'Neill's family tree shows that one of the Great O'Neill's sons, Shane, who later returned to fight in Ireland, had a son, Patrick, Comte de Tyrone, born in 1622, and that his son James went to Martinique. James's son Henry, also Comte de Tyrone, born in 1688, had two sons, Jacques Henri, Comte de Tyrone, and Jean Laurent, Vicomte de Tyrone. Jean Laurent was a captain in the French navy and was recognized by the French king as being a member of the family of the Great O'Neill.

---

* The historical evidence for these assertions seems thin. Micheline Kerney Walsh in *Destruction by Peace, Hugh O'Neill After Kinsale* (Cumann Seanchaí Ard Mhacha, 1986), has traced O'Neill's life after the Flight of the Earls in detail. She writes that the journey of O'Neill and his entourage from Flanders to Rome is well documented and that they travelled from Nancy to Colmar, Basle and Lucerne, and then through Switzerland into Italy. They did not stop at or near Besançon. In addition there is no evidence that Hugh O'Neill left Rome after 1608 and neither is there a record of a son called Shane who went back to fight in Ireland.

Jean Laurent had three sons and they all went into the regiment of Dillon, but we do not know what happened. The problems start there because his brother Jacques Henri, who was an officer in Martinique, had descendants, but they died out in 1932. We do not know where we come. Perhaps Hugh had another son in France or perhaps one of his descendants had. We are all from the area of eastern France – Besançon, Bar-le-Duc, Châlons-sur-Marne.

There was also, from the same area, a Eugene O'Neill who was a soldier in the French army in 1640 and became a marshal. He had two sons, one of whom, Adrian, was a priest to Louis xv. Eugene could have been a son of Hugh or a cousin or from another branch of the great family that left with Hugh, so maybe we came from him.

François O'Neill is convinced of his descent from the Great O'Neill and is continuing his research to prove it. Several years ago he had a party for all the O'Neills in France, of whom there are dozens, and he has drawn up a more modern family tree starting with his grandfather, Auguste O'Neill, who was born in 1829 and was an admiral in the French navy.

We have all been in the navy or in the army. We had three or four admirals and we lost many in the First World War. So we have been moving home all the time. As soon as a war started we were in it but we are finished with the military now. We are all engineers and bankers. My son has left the navy and is joining me in business.

François O'Neill's cousin, Michel O'Neill, was a fighter pilot in the last war and served in North Africa, Tunisia, France and Germany. In his Paris office, from which he runs an aviation consultancy, he has a photo of a crash landing he made in North Africa. Another cousin, Jean O'Neill, practically created the town of Delat in Vietnam, and Marc O'Neill, who died in 1957, was a national hero of the Resistance and a full colonel at the age of thirty-two. When the Algerian War broke out he gave up business and set off to fight again. He was killed there and received a national funeral at Les Invalides. Yet another, Robert O'Neill, was head of one of the biggest banks in France, and Maurice O'Neill was well known in horse-breeding circles.

François O'Neill comes to Ireland practically every year for the shooting and several years ago his daughter married a cousin, another O'Neill, in Connemara.

Richard Hayes states that the O'Neills of Portugal did indeed acquire their designation through an agreement drawn up with the Martinique O'Neills, but he says they are descended from Phelim O'Neill of Killitragh, Co. Derry, the chief of the elder branch of his house who left after the Boyne and was killed with the Irish Brigade at Malplaquet.

The current Lord O'Neill of Shane's Castle, Co. Antrim, is a descendant of the Rev. William Chichester, who changed his surname to that of O'Neill by royal licence in 1855 when he inherited lands belonging to an O'Neill cousin. Lord O'Neill of the Maine, Terence O'Neill, the former Prime Minister of Northern Ireland, is an uncle of the present Lord O'Neill.

The history of the St Leger family could not be more different from that of the O'Neills. While they, too, came to France from Ireland, although nearly 100 years later, served in the French army and now have many members in established positions in and around Paris, they are a Norman family, as opposed to the Gaelic O'Neills, and they were merely returning to the home they had left with William the Conqueror in the eleventh century. In fact one member of the family, Sir Anthony St Leger, who was lord lieutenant from 1540 to 1548, Henry VIII's man in Ireland, pursued the policy of 'Surrender and Regrant' in relation to the Irish chieftains and actually received the submission of Hugh O'Neill's grandfather, Conn Bacach O'Neill.

St Leger is also the family name of the earls of Doneraile, who died out twice but continued through the female line, rent by scandals, strange deaths and local hostility in Co. Cork. Today their lineage is so complicated that the title is open to challenge, and the imposing Doneraile Court has barely survived destruction.

Doneraile was the early eighteenth-century home of the famous lady freemason, Elizabeth St Leger, who fell asleep behind the curtains and awoke to find a highly secret masons' meeting in progress. The masons had no choice but to admit her to the brotherhood.

Doneraile Court was also the scene of the terrible death of the 4th Lord Doneraile, who was killed by a bite from a rabid pet fox which left him delirious in 1887. Lord Doneraile and his coachman, who had also been bitten, travelled to Paris to consult Louis Pasteur, but the viscount grew bored with the treatment, gave it up and developed the disease; his coachman persevered and lived.

Europe's first steeplechase is believed to have been the 1752 race between a Mr O'Callaghan and a Mr Blake over the four-and-a-half miles from the church at Buttevant to Doneraile, with the spire of the St Leger church as a guide. Hence the 'steeple' in chase. The St Leger race, however, one of the five great flat classics which is run annually at Doncaster in England and also in Ireland and France, appears to have got its name from Lieutenant-General Anthony St Leger of Park Hill, near Doncaster, who organized such a race in 1776.

The head of the family in France is Maurice, Vicomte St Leger, and he has amassed much knowledge and documentation on his background. His ancestor was Matthew St Leger, who was born in 1695 and came to France with his elder brother, Anthony, the same year. The boys joined their uncle, Laurence St Leger, who was a follower of James II, and Anthony was entered as a cadet in the Irish regiment of Lee by Louis XIV when he was a mere seven years old in 1696. The vicomte believes the family left Ireland for religious reasons, and the French St Legers, in contrast to the Irish branch, have remained Catholic.

The family were Jacobites and as the boys' great-grandfather, Sir George St Leger, and his eldest son, Patrick, were attainted by the Cromwellian regime in 1653 and again by William of Orange forty years later, it seemed pointless remaining in Ireland. Laurence was killed in the battle of Malplaquet in 1709 and left no children. Both of his nephews fought at Fontenoy where their cousin, Richard St Leger, was killed in 1745 and where the bravery of the Irish Brigades is still remembered.

Matthew, who was killed at Culloden in the following year when he followed Bonny Prince Charlie to Scotland, left eight children and his eldest son, Jean, 1st Baron St Leger, was recognized by Louis XVI as having been Lord of Slievemargy in Queen's County (Laois). Jean was himself taken prisoner at Culloden where his father died but later saw service with the regiments of Bulkeley and Lee in the War of the Austrian Succession. He left two sons, both officer-engineers, and one, Maurice, served under Napoleon and married a Scottish woman, Frances Robertson. Maurice's grandson was the grandfather of the present vicomte.

The family has continued to be associated with the army and, in particular, with the engineering corps. The present vicomte, who was also an engineer, divides his time between his apartment at St Cloud in Paris and his house in Savoy. There are twenty-eight male St Legers in France today, he says. As well as old documents, he has many items associated with his ancestors including the silver seal of the six-year-old Anthony, who came over in 1695.

The ancestral home of the St Legers is at St Leger au Bois, near Ou, but only a dungeon remains. Legend has it that it was Robert St Leger who lent his hand to William the Conqueror as he stepped ashore in Sussex in 1066. Robert's great-great-grandson, William, established the branch of the family that later went to Ireland, when King John gave him estates in Kilkenny and Laois in 1192. His ancestors were loyal servants of the Crown and the Vicomte St Leger has details of the praise they received from Edward II in 1359 for fighting off the O'Moores, MacMurroughs and O'Ryans. Throughout the period they were known as lords of Tullaghanbrogue and barons of Rosconnel.

Almost a century after the first St Legers arrived in France, another family of the same name left from Limerick. Edmund St Leger was a doctor who studied at the Irish College in Paris and was sent as an administrator to the French West Indies during the time of the Revolution. He eventually returned to medical practice in Paris and was followed in this profession by one of his sons. His other son joined the Irish Brigades and saw service in the Napoleonic wars. He retired with the rank of chef de batallion and died in Paris in 1834.

Two families who came to Ireland with the Vikings have also settled in the Paris area – the Plunketts and the Coppingers. The Coppingers are descended from Stephen Coppinger of Ballyvolane, who was Mayor of Cork in the mid-seventeenth century and died in 1660. His great-grandson William was the last Catholic High Sheriff of Cork and, with his three brothers, Thomas, who was outlawed for his loyalty to James II, Henry and Matthew, was attainted for high treason against the English Crown.

William emigrated to Bordeaux where his great-grandson, also William, set up as a leading merchant and married the daughter of Edward Sexton of Limerick. The Coppingers were much involved in trade with the West Indies and lost heavily in the American War.

Their son, James Coppinger, left France during the Revolution and with his wife, Louise Antoinette Dessales, whose family had large estates in Martinique, had nine children, all of them born in Hampstead in England.

James returned after the Restoration and was established as a banker in Paris. His descendants are still resident in the city.

Francis Coppinger, who lives with his wife and family at Neuilly and works in advertising, has an elaborate family tree tracing the progress of the Coppingers, from Stephen of Ballyvolane to the middle of this century. It was compiled by some Canadian Coppingers, and while the French line stops at Paul, Francis's great-grandfather who was a lawyer at the Court of Appeal in Paris, there are some details of the English branch who are also of course descended from Stephen.

The tree shows that Marian, daughter of John Coppinger of Ballyvolane, married the future 12th Duke of Norfolk in 1767 but died in childbirth two years later, and that Richard William Coppinger, who was the staff-surgeon on the royal navy's HMS *Vernon*, had Mount Coppinger and Cape Coppinger in Greenland named after him when he was one of the officers on the Arctic Expedition of 1875-6. His parents were Joseph William Coppinger, a solicitor of Farmley, Dundrum, Co. Dublin, and Agnes Mary Cooke of Fort William, Co. Tipperary.

A Spanish line of Coppingers is descended from Cornelius, the grandson of Henry, one of the four attainted brothers, who was found guilty of harbouring a Catholic priest and forced to leave Cork. His son was General José Coppinger of the Spanish army.

The Coppingers came to England from Denmark in 860 and in 1250 one Nicholas Koppinger was Mayor of Winchester. The first Coppinger found in Ireland was Adam, who was living there in 1308. While William Coppinger emigrated with the Stuarts, the elder branch remained at Ballyvolane. Coppinger Court, near Clonakilty, Co. Cork, is now a ruin and Ballyvolane itself, the family home, was demolished some years ago.

Patrice de Plunkett, chief editor of *Figaro* magazine and one of the best-known writers on the arts in France, is descended from the Plunketts of north-west Co. Dublin, who left Ireland in the early eighteenth century to join the imperial army of Austria. His ancestors were officers in the Napoleonic wars and after spending some time in Brussels they moved to France during the reign of Napoleon III. Irish officers were held in particular regard by the Austrians and it was easier to reach high rank in the imperial army than elsewhere.

M. de Plunkett says the family papers were mislaid during several wars and they are unsure of much of their background. He does know that their branch was called Knockria and that while they are only distant relations of the Dunsany Plunketts of Co. Meath, they are connected to Brigit Mary Plunkett who was born in Louvain in 1757, the daughter of Thomas Plunkett, baron of the Austrian empire and lieutenant-general of the Austrian army.

When lady-in-waiting to the Duchess of Orléans, wife of Philippe Egalité, Mary Brigit married the Marquis de Chastellux. Although imprisoned as an aristocrat during the Revolution, she escaped the guillotine, unlike her kinswoman Elizabeth Plunkett, who lost her head for her royalist beliefs during the terror at Arras in north-eastern France in 1794.

I think Miss Plunkett, the Marquise de Châtellux, was probably a cousin. A part of our family had settled in Lorraine but this branch disappeared during the first half of the nineteenth century. After we left Austria we spent some time in Brussels and then moved to France. My great-grandfather was the owner of the theatre at the Palais Royale and he discovered Offenbach and Schneider. My grandfather burned the family papers in the early days of the First World War because we were Austrians and because he was left-wing – in our class of people that was unusual – and because there was a patriotic crisis at the time.

There are a number of years about the installation of the first Plunketts in Vienna around 1760 that we do not know of, and my parents are trying to find out some details in the military academy. We had one or two generals and several of the family were killed in different wars – one at the battle of Montebello and another by the Prussians in the nineteenth century.

Patrice de Plunkett is known in France for his best-selling book *La Culture en Vest Rose* – an analysis of arts policy under socialist government.

> I was against socialist policy on culture. I think culture is not and must not be a government matter. I think the idea of rightist culture or leftist culture is wrong. Does it mean anything? Culture exists or it does not. Right and left on cultural issues is nonsense. The problem in society is its survival, not its involvement in political fights.

The Irish College at rue des Irlandais on the Left Bank, close to the Sorbonne, is today the centre of Irish interest in Paris, as it was for long periods over the last 400 years. Fr Liam Swords, the *proviseur et aumônier*, writes in his short history, *Soldiers, Scholars, Priests*, that the Paris Irish College was the first, the largest and the most lasting of some thirty Irish Colleges spread across Europe by the end of the eighteenth century.

Founded by a Waterford merchant, John Lee, in 1578, it was originally sited at Collège de Montaigu and later at the Italian Collège des Lombards. Once at rue des Irlandais, however, it opened its doors to include students not destined for the priesthood but studying such disciplines as medicine and the law. Pupils came from both the large Irish community in France, many with families in the Irish Brigades, and from Ireland.

During the Revolution it became, for some time, a prison and interned within its walls some Irish students who had failed to escape the Terror of 1793-4. Two of the principals, Dr John Baptist Walsh and Abbé Charles Kearny, narrowly escaped the guillotine when they were denounced by some of their students as counter-revolutionaries. The endowment of Maynooth saw a falling-off in enrolments.

With the exception of the period 1914-18, Irish clerical students continued to attend the College up to the Second World War, when it was taken over for a time by the United States military. In 1945 a group of Poles acquired a lease on the large building and it became a Polish seminary. In recent years the Poles ran a school for young emigrés but it is now being extensively renovated by a FÁS team, with the help of a Committee in Ireland and the Dublin government. The ownership is complicated.

As with all other Church buildings, the College was confiscated by the state during the Revolution and when Napoleon came to power he established a *Bureau Gratuit* to administer it for the French government. This trust still operates today and is composed mainly of senior civil servants from various departments. Fr Swords believes that if it were not for this body, which prevented the Irish selling their interest, and the occupancy of the Poles, which prevented the French allocating the building to other purposes, the College would very likely have been disposed of years ago, a fate that befell other Irish Colleges on the Continent.

The Poles still have their lease and occupy the larger part of the building, but a small section is being renovated for the Irish. A statue of Wolfe Tone, who spent so much time in Paris gathering support for his homeland, is to be erected in the grounds, and it is intended that the College will again become a centre of learning and a home for Irish students in Paris.

44: Château Dillon

45: Tellières-le-Pléssis

46: Château
d'Arasse

TWELVE

THE IRISH BRIGADES

The Dillons

T HE DILLONS were probably the best known of all the Irish families in France in the seventeenth and eighteenth centuries because of their continuing pre-eminence in the Irish Brigades, of which they were hereditary commanders and colonels.

Mercenary armies were the norm in the Europe of the time. Rich or adventurous officers recruited soldiers into regiments which often bore their names. Although these forces were generally raised for a particular purpose and held an allegiance to one state or king, occasionally they switched sides.

The outbreak of the French Revolution in 1789 caused great confusion among the Irish regiments, which found themselves in a dilemma as to whether to support the French Crown, whose assistance to the Stuarts had often led them to France in the first place, or the new Republic.

---

44   CHÂTEAU DILLON, BORDEAUX *Late 17th-century, originally known as the Château de Terrefort, acquired, restored and renamed in 1753 by the banker Robert Dillon, father of 'Le Beau Dillon'. Now the property of a wine co-operative, the chais are restored but the château has been abandoned.*

45   TELLIÈRES-LE-PLÉSSIS *Elegant 18th-century country retreat in the Orne valley. Seat of the Lismullen branch of the Dillons.*

46   CHÂTEAU D'ARASSE *Sited in a remote valley, dating from 1682. Burnt during the Revolution, rebuilt a year before the 1848 revolution in the so-called 'style troubadour' or early gothic revival and remains unchanged. Gives private meaning to Antoine de Saint-Exupéry's novel* Flight to Arras.

Many officers, some taking their regiments with them, went abroad to join the emigré princes and fight for a return of the Bourbons. Others stayed and fought in the armies of the Republic. Some even went so far as to recruit in Ireland for the British army with a view to fighting in Europe against the new French regime. Instead they were sent to the West Indies where they died of disease in their hundreds.

In their early days the Irish Brigades were recruited in Ireland. Later only their officers were Irish or the sons of Irish. Many started in this career when they fought for James II and then found themselves attainted and without hope after the Boyne and Limerick. Their country was defeated and, even had they cared to, as Catholics they were not permitted to join the British army.

They left Ireland, officers and men, because the Treaty of Limerick gave them that option, because they believed that a Stuart victory would end the terrible penalties imposed on their homeland and introduce religious freedom, and because there was no future for them at home. It is estimated that half-a-million Irishmen died on foreign battlefields between the Treaty of Limerick of 1691 and the French Revolution a hundred years later.

The war between the two kings, William and James, for the throne of England, which had been won by William in Ireland, continued on the Continent. When the Stuarts lost again in Europe some Irish continued to fight for them, going to Scotland with Prince Charles Edward and tasting defeat yet again at Culloden. Others took up the standard of the Bourbons. Either way, the great days of the Irish Brigades were practically over in 1791 when the revolutionary powers in France, who distrusted foreigners in general and royalists in particular, disbanded the remnants of a force which after all had started out as a Jacobite army.

The Irish Brigades in France consisted of numerous regiments which changed their names with the change of proprietor. At various stages, and for various lengths of time between 1647 and 1815, the Brigades, which in the early days at least overlapped with the Jacobite army, included the following regiments: York's, the Earl of Bristol's, Lord Muskerry's (MacCarthy), Lord Mountcashel's (MacCarthy), Lord Clare's (O'Brien), Viscount Galmoy's (Butler), Bourke's, the Duke of Berwick's (Fitzjames), Dornington's, Albemarle's, Sheldon's, Lee's, O'Brien's, Nugent's, Lally's, Rothe's, Bulkeley's, Walsh's, Conway's, and, even after disbandment, O'Connell's (which fought for England at one stage), O'Moran's (defeated in Saint-Domingue), and the Duc de Feltre's (Clark), which served under Napoleon. Throughout practically the whole period there was a Dillon regiment in existence.

The first Irish regiment of the century to go into exile was probably that raised by the Wall brothers of Waterford, who in 1632 took 3000 men to fight for Louis XIII. The brothers, sons of Gerard Wall of Coolnamuck – Michael, Richard, Edmund and Gerard – were all killed in the service of France. A short time later Charles II of England, a refugee on the Continent during the regime of Cromwell, formed an exile army under the protection of the French which included York's, Bristol's, Muskerry's and Dillon's regiments.

The real history of the Irish Brigades begins in 1688, however, when James II fled from London to France on the advance of his son-in-law, William of Orange, and four years later when Patrick Sarsfield, 1st Earl of Lucan, and defender of Limerick, took 12,000 men to France hoping, eventually, to gather an army to launch an invasion of Ireland.

There were now two Irish armies in France, Sarsfield's men fighting for and under James, although paid by the French, and the 20,000-strong Irish Brigades fighting for Louis XIV and divided into three regiments named after their commanders, Lord Mountcashel's (Justin MacCarthy), Lord Clare's (Daniel O'Brien), and Arthur Dillon's.

Most of this second force had come to France under the bizarre arrangement of 1690 whereby Louis xiv sent a 6000-strong veteran army to Ireland under the Comte de Lauzun and the same ships left Cork for France with 5000 Irish recruits.

Within five years, however, more than one third of both Irish armies were injured or dead, the planned invasions of Ireland and of England, which many exiles hoped for, had been abandoned, and Sarsfield himself had been killed at the 1693 battle of Landen in the Low Countries, apparently with the words "Would it were for Ireland" on his lips.

William had now won the war on the Continent and at the Treaty of Ryswick of 1697 Louis xvi recognized him as King of England. As a consequence James was no longer allowed to have an army and the Jacobite force was drastically cut back. More or less abandoned by both James and Louis, some of these 12,000 Irish troops, who had arrived so hopefully to fight for the Stuart restoration seven years earlier, were absorbed into various French units or, being unemployed, emigrated to fight for other states. The peace did not last long and the War of the Spanish Succession soon presented numerous opportunities for Wild Geese all over Europe. Peter Lacy of Limerick, for example, entered the army of Peter the Great of Russia, fought in Sweden, Poland, the Crimea and Finland, and rose to the rank of field-marshal in 1736.

The Irish Brigades, however, continued to fight for France and some regiments distinguished themselves, notably at Cremona in 1701, where Daniel O'Mahony of Dillon's saved the French army; at Luzara where several thousand Irishmen died: at Blenheim, at Ramillies and at Malplaquet. Four regiments of the Brigades – Dillon's, Rothe's, Lally's and Fitzjames's – fought at Culloden, having been dispatched by Louis. After the defeat they were treated as French rather than as rebels and returned to the Continent.

In 1745 the Irish Brigades had their greatest triumph at Fontenoy. The Irish troops are said to have cried, "Cuimhnighidh ar Luimneach agus ar fhéile na Sasanaigh" (Remember Limerick and the Saxon faith), as they marched into battle and saved the day. On hearing of the defeat of his son, the Duke of Cumberland, George II is reported to have said, "Cursed be the laws which deprive me of such subjects."

It is ironic that in these battles which raged across Europe, and now had little or no connection with the Stuart cause, Irishmen in the French army were fighting Irishmen in the imperial army. Casualties were enormous and recruits from Ireland declined dramatically as the Stuarts went from one failure to another and the French executed General Lally. Occasional desertions from the Austrian force filled the gap, but with the decline in Jacobite prospects towards the end of the century only the officers in the Brigades tended to be Irish.

In 1756 a regiment of the Irish Brigades was sent to India to protect French interests against the British. Its commander was Thomas Arthur Lally, the French-born son of Sir Gerald Lally of Tullynadala, Co. Galway, whose lands had been confiscated in 1691. Known in France as Lally Tollendal, Lally was first a member of Dillon's but later formed his own regiment and served with distinction in many battles, including Fontenoy, before being appointed commander-in-chief of the Indian expedition.

After initial successes he was defeated at Wandiwash and taken captive by the Limerick-born English commander, Eyre Coote, at Pondicherry. Back in France, after a time as a prisoner in England, he was beheaded by the French for having lost them India. The judgment against him was later reversed through the efforts of his son, Trophime Gerard.

In 1779 Dillon's regiment, with some members of Walsh's and some French, was sent to the West Indies and to America where they fought well, but during this period the Brigade was being gradually disbanded. It was dissolved, although other regiments later appeared, by a decree of the National Assembly in 1791. At this stage France was in turmoil and the Brigade itself was split between royalists and republicans.

The story of the Dillons illustrates how many noble Irish families fared during the century. James Dillon of the Dillon family of Costello-Gallen of Cos Mayo and Roscommon, was born in 1600 and left for France with the second flight of Wild Geese after the Cromwellian campaign in Ireland in which he had served on the Irish side. He formed the first Dillon regiment, rose to the rank of major-general in the French force, and fought in the Flanders campaign. His regiment was disbanded when he died in 1664.

His kinsman the 7th Viscount Dillon, Theobald, fought with James II and was outlawed by the English in 1690. His second son, Arthur, who was born in Roscommon in 1670, went as a colonel of a new regiment of Dillon's with Lord Mountcashel's Brigade in 1690. He served in the Spanish, German and Italian campaigns and rose to the rank of commander-in-chief of the army of the Rhine. He was close to the Old Pretender, Jacques III, and involved in several schemes for a Stuart restoration. He was created Comte Dillon by Louis XIV in 1711 and Earl Dillon by the Old Pretender in 1721. He died at the Stuart court in St Germain-en-Laye in 1733.

Arthur left five sons, one of whom, Charles, abandoned France and returned to Ireland when he inherited the estates and title of Lord Dillon from his cousin in 1737. He was succeeded as 11th Viscount by his brother Henry, who also resigned his commission as colonel in the French army. Henry married Lady Charlotte Lee and their son Charles conformed to the Protestant religion and was confirmed as 12th Viscount by the English House of Lords in 1788. This branch of the family lived for several generations in England where they inherited Ditcheley (one of the grandest houses in England, now a centre for Anglo-American studies) from the Lees, but they returned to Ireland in the 1950s and lived in Co. Louth until 1983. The present Lord Dillon was born in 1973 and lives in London.

Arthur's third son, James, was killed at Fontenoy at the head of the Dillon regiment, and the fourth son, Edward, next colonel of Dillon's, was killed at Lauffelt two years later. The fifth son was a cleric who became the rich and famous Archbishop of Narbonne, architect of much of the city. Henrietta-Lucy Dillon, Madame de la Tour du Pin (see Chapter One), his grandniece, had interesting things to say about his household where she spent much of her youth.

> In my earliest years [she writes in her *Memoirs*] I saw things which might have been expected to warp my mind, pervert my affections, deprave my character and destroy in me every notion of religion and morality. From the age of ten, I heard around me the freest conversations and the expression of the most ungodly principles. Brought up, as I was, in an Archbishop's house where every rule of religion was broken daily, I was fully aware that my lessons in dogma and doctrine were given no more importance than those in history and geography.

A life-size portrait of the archbishop hangs at Newbridge House, Donabate, Co. Dublin. It came to the Cobbes, owners of Newbridge, several years ago when Isabelle Dillon, aunt of the present Lord Dillon, married into the family.

Arthur, the younger son of Henry, 11th Lord Dillon, and brother to Charles, the 12th Viscount, became colonel and proprietor of the regiment in 1767 when he was only seventeen years old. He served in the American War of

Independence and in the French West Indies and was elected deputy for Martinique in the National Assembly. He is reputed to have saved France at Valmy in 1792 when the Austrian army was poised to move on Paris.

Although an aristocrat and prominent among those who argued against the execution of Louis XVI, he escaped the early days of the Terror but was arrested in 1794 and brought before the Revolutionary Tribunal. Charged with conspiring against the national safety, attempting to destroy the National Convention and plotting to restore the monarchy by rescuing the Dauphin, he was found guilty and guillotined.

This Arthur Dillon left two daughters. The first, by his marriage to Lucie Rothe of the Kilkenny family who formed Rothe's regiment, became the Comtesse de la Tour du Pin and author of the celebrated *Memoirs*. His second daughter, Fanny, by his marriage to the Comtesse de la Touche, a first cousin of the Empress Josephine, married General Bertrand, one of Napoleon's officers who accompanied him to St Helena and remained with him until his death.

A relative of these Costello-Gallen Dillons, Theobald Dillon, born in Dublin in 1745, emigrated with his family to Orléans when his father's bank failed. He joined the Dillon regiment, served in America and reached the rank of general in the French service when the Irish regiment was amalgamated into it. He was murdered by his own troops during a mêlée in Lille in 1792 when panic set in over a report that the Austrian army was advancing.

Meanwhile Theobald's uncle, Robert Dillon, had set up as a banker in Bordeaux and established himself at Château Dillon, or Terrefour, which he bought in 1753 and where he lived in much splendour for several years. Wine is still produced at the château by the Lycée Agricole de Bordeaux, and while the *chais* are in full use the château itself is abandoned and has been dilapidated for some fifteen years.

Robert's son Edward, known as Le Beau Dillon, was born in Bordeaux in 1751, entered Dillon's regiment and saw service in America and the colonies. He frequented the court of Louis xvi and Marie Antoinette, and Richard Hayes reports that his relationship with the doomed queen was rumoured to have been more than platonic. On the outbreak of Revolution he joined the emigré princes abroad and with his brothers tried to form a new Dillon regiment to fight the republican army, which included the recently disbanded Dillon regiment led by his cousin Theobald.

When this attempt failed, Edward Dillon and other royalist Irish officers attempted, with some success, to raise a force in Ireland to serve against France as part of the British army. He commanded this regiment until 1810 and on the Restoration became a French ambassador. He and his two brothers bore the title of comte because their father had been admitted to the French nobility.

Several other Dillons also served in various French armies, including the Earl of Roscommon, the engineer James Vincent Dillon, who built the first Pont des Arts in Paris, and Peter Dillon, who was guillotined by the Revolutionary Tribunal in Nantes.

A privately published history of the Dillons in France has been written by the Marquis de Certaines, whose wife is Bridget Dillon of the Terrefour family. He lists seven noble Dillon houses with French connections. The family of the Lords Dillon of Costello-Gallen, descendants of the Jacobite Arthur Dillon who led the regiment to France with Mountcashel in 1690, are Lords Dillon in England and Comtes Dillon in France; the descendants of the Terrefour Dillons, of Edward le Beau Dillon and his brothers, are the Comtes Dillon de France; the Dillons of Lismullen, Co. Meath, are represented by the Dillon-Cornecks; the Dillons of Balgeeth are represented by Vicomte Jacques Dillon who lives in Paris; the Lords of Roscommon have died out, as have the Barons Dillon of Clonbrock.

The Dillon-Cornecks, whose family home is at Château Tellières-le-Pléssis in Orne, west of Paris, are descended from Sarah Millicent Dillon of Lismullen, Co. Meath, a branch of the Roscommon Dillons, who married Thomas Corneck of Cornwall in 1815. Lismullen was destroyed during the Troubles in Ireland seventy years ago and later partly rebuilt. It is now owned by Opus Dei.

Millicent's descendant, Robert Dillon-Corneck, lives today with his Australian wife and his daughter in an elegant apartment on the Left Bank in Paris. He has a cottage in Kerry and travels to Ireland frequently. His elder brother, Jacques, lives at Tellières-le-Pléssis.

In the far south of France are other Dillons who are unaware of any connection with the military Dillons. The Baron Patrick Dillon Kavanagh de Feartagh is obviously Irish, but knows little of his own background. A gentleman farmer and bachelor, he lives in a rambling old château near Agen, a large town on the Garonne between Bordeaux and Toulouse, with its rooms unchanged since their neo-medieval redecoration in the nineteenth century. He is a charming, hospitable, large, Irish-looking man who speaks no English. His brother and family farm nearby.

Apart from saying that his ancestor came to France from Ireland at the time of Mary Stuart, which would indicate an unusual early support for the family, Patrick Dillon Kavanagh de Feartagh knows nothing of his Irish ancestry. Mary Stuart, daughter of James v of Scotland and Mary of Guise, was Queen of France during the short reign of her husband Francis II (1559-60) and Queen of Scotland from her birth in 1542 until her son James VI (later James I of England) replaced her. The baron knows his title de

Feartagh is Irish (it means of the mound and is a common designation) and believes his ancestor first settled at Laval in Mayenne.

The Marquis de Certaines, however, gives a slightly different version. He writes in his family history that Patrick Julian Dillon Kavanagh, Lord de Feartagh, arrived in France at the beginning of the eighteenth century to escape the persecution of the Catholics in Ireland. Although many of the family papers were destroyed in Ireland and the remainder lost in France during the First World War, the Kavanaghs were ancient kings of Leinster and the genealogist O'Hart thinks, according to de Certaines, that the de Feartaghs could be descended from a branch of the family of Sir Moroch Kavanagh who emigrated from Carlow to France after the Boyne in 1690.

In any case Patrick Julian and his wife, who was a Butler, had a son, Arthur (1758-1820), who became commander of the ports for the king. Arthur's great-grandson, George Arthur, moved to south-west France from Mayenne. He was, his grandson the present baron says, an Olympic champion in fencing and was the representative in France for the Bugatti car company.

The present baron's mother is Suzanne de Saint-Exupéry and it is through her that the Château d'Arasse came to the Dillon Kavanaghs. Set deep in rolling agricultural land, it has remained untouched for many years. Originally built in 1682, it was burnt during the Revolution and reconstructed in 1847. As the home of the baron's late grandfather, the Marquis de Saint-Exupéry, whose family acquired it by marriage four generations previously, Saint-Exupéry crests are much in evidence and there is little of the Dillon Kavanaghs to be seen. As in other châteaux in France, many of the walls are decorated with engravings of the French kings.

Coincidentally it was at nearby Toulouse that, according to Hayes, the last known sighting of the ancient gold crown of the Kavanaghs occurred. Hayes writes that Nicholas Kavanagh, who was living in Nantes in 1776, whence his father had fled from Carlow after the Williamite confiscations, was regarded in France as the representative of the kings of Leinster. The crown, which the family still possessed, was last seen at an exhibition or museum in Toulouse just before the Revolution. All efforts to trace it have failed.

47: GOULAINE

THIRTEEN

THE IRISH BRIDE

The O'Briens and the Blosse Lynchs

W HEN THE GERMANS came to the Château de Goulaine during the last war with the intention of making it their Nantes headquarters, the cousin of the marquis, whose home it then was, made sure they knew of its unique geographical position on a site that has kept it in the one family for a thousand years without even a burning. It is bordered on three sides by marshes and semi-circular canals, and on the fourth by the Loire. The only sure entry is up the long tree-lined avenue over the marsh.

Partisans, the officers were told, could easily cut it off and a military map was produced to emphasize the point. The Germans left and never returned. The château was saved once more.

Today's Marquis de Goulaine, the 11th, is the owner of the Château de Goulaine in more senses than one. Not only does it bear his name, and the name of the well-known Muscadet wine he produces, but he bought it from his cousin in 1957 by selling practically everything he had to raise the cash. It came about thus: the marquis's great-grandfather had been given a choice of two properties when he came into his inheritance and he chose La Grange, which had been recently modernized in the Victorian fashion. His younger brother got Goulaine and when his descendant decided to sell it in 1957 the present marquis, who was living

---

47 GOULAINE *One of fortresses guarding approach to Nantes and Brittany. Earliest surviving part is the 15th-century three-sided courtyard with gatehouse on the fourth. Two staircase towers and dormers are highly sculptured. Wings were remodelled during reign of Louis XIII with sumptuous interiors in blue and gold and treasures disrupted by war and divisions of legacies.*

in La Grange, knew he had to buy it. "I was twenty-three years old. I had just lost my father. I thought I could not let it go out of the family. It cost me all my fortune."

Since then he has been building a business around the château. It is open to the public and can be rented for weddings, exhibitions, seminars and dinners. It is also the centre of a thriving butterfly farm and the franchise thereof, and it is the home of Marquis de Goulaine wine.

The château had had a narrow escape even earlier than the last war. The year before the French Revolution of 1789 the family ran out of money and sold Goulaine to a Dutch banker from Nantes. Many fortunes were being made in Nantes from the slave trade at the time, as in other Atlantic-coast cities such as Bordeaux and Bristol, and a buyer was easy to find. As a foreigner, the Dutchman was remote from the Revolution and took the side of neither republicans nor royalists. The protagonists, who were particularly fierce in this area of La Vendée, respected this and left him and his château alone.

Of the three Goulaines of that time, two were guillotined and the other died in exile. One of those guillotined left two children, a two-year-old boy and a girl of four, and they were hidden in the woods by a gamekeeper until danger had passed. The boy grew up to be Alphonse, Marquis de Goulaine, and he married Henrietta Galwey of the well-known Cork family. Their son Patrice bought back the castle and land.

Several members of the Galwey family, who were Jacobites, had moved to France and to Nantes in particular, as a result of the confiscations that followed the Treaty of Limerick. They were wine-traders, known in France as *négotiants*, and part of the marquis's Irish blood, which is not very strong, comes from this union. The rest is on his mother's side.

The marquis unfolds a huge circular genealogical tree (the way it should be done, he says) containing the names of hundreds of ancestors. It shows that the first Galwey to come to Nantes was André and his wife Helena Kavanagh, and that their granddaughter was Henrietta who in 1820 married Alphonse de Goulaine.

His mother's side of the circle – she was Charlotte d'Argenson – shows descent from Antoinette O'Brien de Thomond, whose father was the 6th Viscount Clare. Clare, Charles O'Brien, commanded the Irish Brigade regiment of the same name, and for bravery on the field, including Fontenoy, he became one of three Irishmen to be made marshals of France. (The others were MacMahon, Duc de Magenta, and Clarke, Duc de Feltre.) Antoinette married the Duc de Choiseul-Praslin in 1758. One descendant was the duke of the same name who lived in the Château de Vaux le Vicomte,* near Mélun, and who murdered his wife in her bedroom in 1847 – "he was condemned to death but we think he never did it," says the Marquis – and another is the Marquis de Goulaine himself. Also descended from the O'Briens is the Marquis de Breteuil who maintains the Château de Breteuil, thirty-five kilometres south of Paris.

The Galweys fled from Ireland and had a little château near La Flèche. On my mother's side I am a descendant of Brian Boru and his descendant Viscount Clare who came to France with the Wild Geese and, like the Galweys, was recognized as a nobleman. On the Clare side many of the girls are called Slanie or Slaney, which comes from the river

But I am very Celtic on my father's side because we are Bretons. France started at the end of the avenue so we were right on the border. The safety of the border was maintained by three châteaux – Nantes, Goulaine and Clissant.

There is a very deep sentimental connection between Ireland and France. Every time I go I feel at home. It is probably the Celtic style – we are faithful, courageous and unpredictable. The Irish are probably even more so because of the terrible life they had.

---

* Vaux le Vicomte is the most imposing private château in France. It was commissioned by the politician Fouquet from the architect Le Vau, the painter Lebrun and the gardener Le Nôtre, but in 1661 Louis XIV threw their master into prison and transferred the team to Versailles.

The Irish Châteaux

The marquis is proud that he is the twenty-ninth generation traced from father to son, but he is an exceptionally busy and highly successful businessman. He has three jobs, he says: his wine, of which he produces 300,000 bottles a year; his château, with its two-and-a-half acres of roof, a constant stream of visitors and its many functions; and his butterfly farm.

> Wine is my main business. We have been wine-growers for an eternity. We are probably the oldest in the world. I am waiting for someone to deny it. We have been here for a thousand years and all that time we have been growing vines. But I am really the man who made a business out of it. Seventy-five per cent is export; mostly to the US and to Ireland.

There are few items of Irish interest in the château, apart from a portrait of Henrietta and a book he found in his library belonging to a

> 'Mr O'Shea, a gentleman of the king'. It is a genealogy of the O'Cruoly (sic), written by Thady O'Dineen in the mid-eighteenth century. I must be related to them. It is divided into three parts, one Latin, one Gaelic and one French. It says in the Latin preface, 'This is to certify that I, Thady O'Dineen, hereditary genealogist of Ireland, have truly written this genealogy of the O'Cruoly family going backwards in time preferring, so to speak, to be wrong with the historians of my own nation than to be right with the historians of other nations.' I like that.

The butterfly farm, which he started in a section of the château offices in 1984, has been an enormous success.

> I send them to exhibitions everywhere and people come to see them here. They only live for fifteen days so there are 200 flying around at a time. They have helped me a lot because it is my trademark and I am known by butterflies, the château and the wine.

As well as the farm at Goulaine and a breeding centre in Guernsey owned jointly with a friend, the marquis is franchizing the butterfly farm system and has plans to install one on the ninth floor of a Paris store. In the Goulaine greenhouse magnificent species from all corners

160

of the earth fly around aimlessly during their few days of life. A map on the wall identifies their country of origin.

The marquis and his German wife live in the private section of the vast château. They have two sons, one of whom is interested in butterflies, the other in wine. The busy offices, where there is a constant hum of activity, and the greenhouse, are in a cluster of low modern buildings to one side. The family crest is much in evidence.

> Our coat-of-arms is extraordinary because it is the royal coat-of-arms of England and France together. This is because in the twelfth century we were asked by the Pope to act as ambassadors to establish the peace between the kings of France and England who were fighting here. Matthew de Goulaine was so successful that the King of England offered him land and money. He refused and then the king said there is one thing you cannot refuse me, my coat-of-arms – the leopard. And the French king said the same, so we got the leopard and the *fleur-de-lis*.
>
> Our motto is by Abélard who was born only a few miles from here, at Le Pallet – 'Between this king and that king I will establish the peace'.

The Goulaines, he says, are unusual in that when Henry IV, the first Bourbon, gave them their title in the sixteenth century, the document stated that it could descend through the female line. "It was probably because of the Brehon law."

Women have played a large part in the history of the family and he mentions the most famous Yolande de Goulaine. She is depicted with a sword or dagger in her hand because in the Middle Ages, when her father was on the crusades, the English attacked the château and the garrison prepared to surrender. She threatened to kill herself if they did so. They changed their minds, fought on and the château was saved.

> Then there was Anne Mary de Goulaine, a Benedictine nun in the seventeenth century. She was the person who, through her confessor, persuaded King Louis XIII to put France under the special protection of the Holy Virgin. This is the origin of Assumption Day in France, the holiday of August 15th.

Far removed from the Marquis de Goulaine, on the other side of France and in a vastly different château, is another marquis whose female ancestor was also Irish, although from a later date. In a landscape very like that of Co. Wicklow, near the middle of the Massif Central, stands the remote Château de Fournels, dominating a small town of the same name. It is an old medieval fort with its three towers overlooking the three valleys it guards. It's far from anywhere and can only be reached by twisting, narrow and empty roads which criss-cross an almost barren plateau. Beautiful in the heat of central France's summer, it is so bitterly cold and isolated in winter that the area is now being developed for winter sports.

Inside Château de Fournels lives the Marquis de Brion, a bachelor in his eighties whose grandmother was Alice Blosse Lynch, from a family that still live at Partry, Co. Mayo. He has perfect English from his days at Harrow, and he exudes an old-fashioned charm and concern that is rare to meet nowadays. His welcome is so genuine, as is his generosity, that one suspects few travellers pass his way. He talks interestingly, elegantly and speedily of his life as a child during the First World War and as a prisoner of war in the Second, of his uncle the German writer and scholar Count Harry von Kessler, of the *beau monde* in which his uncle mixed and of which he wrote, of the famous people he knew and of his Irish cousins on his mother's side and the Napoleonic duke, Duroc, on his father's.

His château, so imposing from the distance of the road that one would think it would easily withstand an army,

---

48   FOURNELS *Built in 1573 by Jean d'Apicier with three towers and a stone slated roof. Inherited and extended a century later by the Lastic family, whose heiress married a de Brion. 17th- and 18th-century interiors have traces of later romanticism in the painted vaults of the reception rooms. Bust of the grandmother of present Marquis de Brion, portrayed in frothy marble as a belle-époque beauty, overlooks staircase of winding stone.*

48: Fournels

49: Marquis de Brion

50: Salon, Fournels

is sadly in great disrepair but, with some help from the government, plans are afoot at least to re-roof it. None the less the family portraits, the parquet floors, the little office up the stone spiral staircase of the tower, the elegant furniture and magnificent tapestries that adorn rooms where ceilings have partially collapsed, show the former and restorable magnificence. As in so many old French châteaux, the *fleur-de-lis* adorns the walls but here many have been painted straight on to stone and are now chipped. Unfortunately there are no heirs to make the restoration a more pressing matter.

The marquis is frequently referred to as the Duc de Frioul but this is not, he tells us, correct. His grandmother did not like Napoleonic titles and insisted that the family's older designation, which was theirs directly, was preferable. Hence he is the Marquis de Brion.

His grandmother Alice Lynch was born in Bombay where her father, the Mayo man, was a naval officer. With her sister she came to Paris at the turn of the century and married Count von Kessler, a Swiss who took German nationality when he inherited a bank in Hamburg. The couple had a son and a daughter. The daughter, for whom Kaiser Wilhelm stood as godfather, married the Marquis de Brion and the son, known as the Red Count, became well known around Europe.

This Count von Kessler, the marquis's uncle, was a soldier, diplomat, diarist, pacifist, art collector, publisher, traveller and socialite. *The Diaries of a Cosmopolitan*, which cover the years 1918-37, are still read today. He was the first director of the Bauhaus in Weimar, the German design school.

As a German, Von Kessler's fortune was impounded by the British during the First World War, and his priceless art collection was seized by Germany when he died in 1937. The marquis has taken several unsuccessful lawsuits against both governments, the last one only a few years ago, to try and recover some of this inheritance or at least be compensated for its loss. "We have lost everything," he says, more sad than bitter. "The paintings belonged to us as my uncle's heirs. Now they are all, including many by Munch, in museums."

The Duc de Frioul, an Italian honour, was bestowed on the marquis's cousin, Duroc, by Napoleon to whom he was grand marshal of the palaces. A great friend of the emperor, the two men are buried beside each other in Les Invalides. Duroc died twelve hours after being wounded at the battle of Lutzen in Silesia in 1813, and a large painting showing Napoleon visiting him on his deathbed hangs at Fournels. In the drawing-room there is a silver coconut, with lid, which was a present from the emperor.

Following the death of his friend, whom he had known since the early days in Toulon, Napoleon made Frioul's daughter a duchess in her own right. She died, unwed, at seventeen and the title passed to her cousin, the Marquis de Brion, grandfather of the present marquis. It is no longer used.

The marquis is full of information about his family background, his life and his adventures during the last war. He is unusual in France in that he brought up the subject of the war and spoke easily about it. Leaving his Paris publishing business in charge of his sister-in-law, he was conscripted into the French army. His service began in Lorraine but, retreating across France, ended not long afterwards when he was taken prisoner in Brittany.

> People laugh at my war times because the things I did were so strange and comical rather than tragical. We had a general who had 'folie de grandeur' and he had, besides all his military cars, a wine car which was enormous. Every night on the retreat we found a different château to sleep in. They had all been abandoned. I enjoy the funny things. Once we found a very pretty country house and we stayed two or three days. We opened the cupboards

and found many dresses from the end of the nineteenth century. We all dressed up in hats and feathers and at that very moment we were bombarded.

The marquis said he and his regiment, which was loosely organized as it kept being joined by other troops who had lost theirs, were woken each morning by the guns of the advancing Germans. Imprisoned in Laval, he secured his release by falsifying papers which maintained he was a member of the Red Cross.

> I can't say being a prisoner of war was awful because I gave English lessons to the other prisoners and I spoke German and that pleased them and they took me as an interpreter. Except we were in dormitories and we didn't have enough to eat.

On his escape, the marquis returned to Fournels where he helped the Resistance by continuing to falsify papers. On one occasion he narrowly escaped arrest in Clermont-Ferrand when he was stopped by the Vichy police while carrying a load of forged ration cards. On another, at the end of the war, he hid a German officer who wished to defect but who ran into trouble when, having discarded his uniform, found himself unable to surrender to the British military in civilian clothes. The officer eventually spent two years in a prisoner-of-war camp in Scotland.

The marquis spoke frequently of his grandmother's family, the Lynchs. "Two Lynch brothers from Partry married two Taylour sisters. The Lynchs owned a navigation company in the Near East and their boats were well known on the Tigris at the time."

The Château de Fournels has never been sold since it was built in 1573, although it has changed hands several times through marriage. Now its future is uncertain. "I am the last Marquis de Brion. I have an adopted son but in France he cannot inherit. If only there was a sovereign it could be transferred."

51: De La Bretêche

52: Hôtel de Jarnac

FOURTEEN

ISABELLA

The Journals of Lady Isabella Fitzgerald, Vicomtesse de Rohan Chabot

IN 1984 AN OLD MANUSCRIPT, written in English, came to light in the medieval Château de Lagrange, near Paris, the former home of the reformer Lafayette. The château's present owner, the Comte de Chambrun, found it was the journal, covering the years 1784 to 1825, of a distant connection of his family, Lady Isabella Fitzgerald, Comtesse de Rohan Chabot. He had the manuscript transcribed, and, although it covers only the early part of a turbulent life in turbulent times, it makes fascinating reading. As well as detailing her rather sad, single days, it gives a first-hand account of some of the great events of the period, ranging from the 1798 rebellion in Ireland to the consternation in Paris in 1815 when news of the impending return of Napoleon reached the city. The journal includes descriptions of English politicians during the reign of George III, the life of the French court in exile at Hartwell in Buckinghamshire, the fashions of Restoration France, the household requirements of an aristocratic couple and the dangers of sea travel.

---

51   DE LA BRETÊCHE *18th-century country house near Malmaison presented by Josephine to her companion in prison, the Comtesse de Jarnac.*

52   HÔTEL DE JARNAC, RUE MONSIEUR, PARIS *Built by Legrand for Duc de Rohan's younger brother, Comte de Jarnac, and his Irish wife, Elizabeth Smyth, in the most up-to-date neo-classicism. On a fashionable street, its façade is so understated as to be almost invisible. Grandeur reserved for interior, notably the columned salon. Now the property of M. Primat.*

Lady Isabella Fitzgerald starts her journal with the lines, "I was born in Leinster House in Dublin on the 16th of July 1784." Her father was the 2nd Duke of Leinster and his brother, her uncle, was Lord Edward Fitzgerald, the leading United Irishman, who was arrested just before the outbreak of the 1798 rebellion and who died in prison of his wounds during its suppression.

She takes us through the first half of her life, her childhood at Carton, Co. Kildare, at Leinster House, now the seat of the Irish parliament, and at Frescati on the sea at Blackrock, Co. Dublin; the agony over the rebellion; her family's problems and joys; her time as a débutante in London; her unhappy romance; her marriage to a French emigré noble, the Comte de Rohan Chabot, whose mother was Elizabeth Smyth of Tinna Park, Co. Wicklow; her travels with him as his British regiment moved to Portugal to engage in the Peninsular War; her time as chief lady-in-waiting to Louis Philippe's wife in Paris, and many excitements and dramas of the period.

She started writing her journal in 1806 when she was twenty-two, complaining of illness and living unhappily in Cheltenham; her parents were recently dead and she bemoans her small income of £500 a year. But her younger brother Kildare was now duke, and she clearly points out that hers was the only ducal family in Ireland.

> Till the fatal Rebellion of 1798 we could boast of great popularity and influence in Ireland, arising from the constant efforts of our family to promote the welfare of that country and still more, I believe, from their continual residence there. I can well remember the general joy expressed at the birth of my brother Kildare and the motto on the pin cushion which was embroidered for his christening – 'Not a parent's only, but a Nation's wish.' We never went to the theatres without being cheered and the most distinguished attentions met us whenever we appeared in Dublin.

She had a love for her uncle Lord Edward and much to say of his wife Pamela, whose background was the subject

of great speculation.* Edward, she writes, was not tall but
had blue eyes and regular features.

His manly complexion almost concealed his being slightly marked
with the small pox. He was one of the first to cut his hair short
and leave off powder ... His hair was of a dark brown colour
and had sufficient wave in it to make it sit prettily with little care,
besides constant washing, which Lord Edward was almost the first
to introduce, so that the cropped head, as it was called, became a
party distinction.

Isabella describes Pamela thus:

Rather below the middle stature and her figure was not remarkable
for grace but the form of her head and throat was particularly
beautiful as well as the upper part of her face, and her profile
would have afforded a perfect model of Grecian beauty for the
study of an artist. She was the first person who appeared amongst
us with hair out of powder ... She seldom wore rouge and her
complexion, which by daylight was sallow, became by candlelight
as white as marble.

This formed a beautiful contrast with the animation of her fine
expression and the fire of her fine black eyes. Lively, engaging and
agreeable, nobody ever possessed to a greater degree the power of
pleasing, but she was often the victim of caprice and her temper
was far from good.

Pamela's education we could easily perceive was very superficial;
dancing well, acting and reading French plays seemed to be her
only accomplishments. She did not even write French correctly.
In acting mad scenes she was reckoned by good judges almost to
equal the celebrated Mrs Siddons.

But because of Lord and Lady Edwards' sympathy for the
rebel or republican faction in the years leading to '98,

the very colour of our gowns and ribbons became the subject of
misrepresentation and an object of public attention. Green was
prohibited as disloyal and a single stripe of that colour in Kildare's

* Pamela was the pupil of Madame de Genlis, the lady-in-waiting to the Duchesse
d'Orléans and mistress of her husband Philippe Egalité. She was a tutor to the
Orléans children and it was presumed that Pamela was her child by Egalité. Pamela
had been brought up in England, where Egalité spent much of his youth, and was
later introduced to the French court by Madame de Genlis to teach English to the
Orléans children.

plaid silk cravat was not passed over in silence, tho' my dear father, who hated all party colours and petty distinctions, always urged us to comply with the prejudices of the day. Poor Lord Edward used to laugh at all this and say 'Thank God they cannot change the fact of nature in our Emerald Isle, nor dye the fields and trees orange', which was the colour of the opposite faction.

Lord Edward's arrest created great alarm in the family and in the general unrest it was decided they should leave Carton, first for her aunt Lady Louisa Conolly's neighbouring estate of Castletown, and then for Dublin.

As we sought to take a last view of Carton from the carriage windows we beheld the town of Dunboyne in flames. We now recollected hearing that orders had been issued that day to the military to shoot every straggling peasant who could not instantly give an account of himself and the fear of meeting with some of these victims induced us to pull down the green blinds. At Leixlip we were stopped and obliged to get a passport and here we were shocked by the sight of a dead body placed erect by the soldiers against a cart and covered in derision with green ribbons. On reaching Leinster House we found the extensive stables and offices turned into a barrack for the volunteer corps who regularly mounted guard and performed all their military duties under our windows.

During the three months which we passed in Dublin we seldom stirred out but to dine with Lady St George [the author's maternal grandmother] where large parties of Aristocrats assembled every evening to relate all the horrible events of the day with every aggravating circumstance and to censure the Democrats with all the violence of party rage. My uncle and Pamela were not spared, even in our presence, by these illiberal old politicans, who often drew tears of rage and anguish from my eyes, and I always felt relieved when at 9 o'clock precisely we were compelled to return to our respective houses under pain of being detained all night in the guard house.

The residence of Lady St George in Rutland [now Parnell] Square was on the opposite side of the river and very far from Leinster House. It was always distressing to us having so much of the town to traverse almost daily and we were often exposed to very painful sights. One day we met the funeral procession of Ryan, the civil officer who fell by the hand of Lord Edward. Another we fell in with the body of Lord Mountjoy as it was followed to the grave with all the pomp of military honours.

Lord Edward died in June 1798, seventeen days after his arrest, and Lady Isabella describes the efforts of his brother, Lord Henry, and aunt, Lady Louisa of Castletown, to go and see him on his deathbed at Newgate Prison in Dublin.

In 1805 Isabella left Ireland more or less for good. She stayed for periods with various relations in England, was presented at court and met some of the political and society leaders of the day. Feeling she had exhausted the hospitality of her relations, she took an apartment in Cheltenham and looked forward to the single life. It was here, however, that she had her first romances and later, at her sister Lady Cecilia Foley's house in Worcestershire, that she met her great love, William Henry Lyttleton. Her writings, though couched in the language of the day, tell of her feelings for him and of her despair when he leaves her life. Sadly, we are not told why, or how, her hopes were dashed.

Although now spending much time in the London house of her sister Lady Olivia Kennaird and meeting, through Lord Kennaird, most of the political figures of the day, as well as the French emigrés resident with the Orléans family in England, Isabella complains of being almost permanently unwell. Only the efforts of her two paternal aunts, Lady Bellamont and Lady Sophia Fitzgerald, persuade her out into society.

Sent as an invalid to take the sea air at Brighton, she became friends with the two daughters of Henry Grattan, the parliamentary friend of her father, and her spirits perked up. By the end of the following year, 1809, she was married to her old friend Louis de Chabot, the emigré officer. "In the eyes of the world we appeared to be making a love match," she wrote, while making it plain that her heart still pined for Mr Lyttleton.

Among the most interesting material in the journal are the letters the Comte de Jarnac writes to his son Louis about the dangers of marrying without money. Louis had failed in his efforts to win the heiress Lady Eleanor Butler, daughter of the Marquess of Ormond. "In the eyes of the generality of the world great names unsupported by a fortune, at least sufficient to live with decency according to the rank, are rather turned into contemptuous ridicule." He continues by listing what he believes indispensable for the couple to survive on a moderate scale – a house in town for six months, two living-in servants, four maids including a cook, and job-horses and coachman for three months each year.

Louis, of course, had no money, the Jarnac fortune and estates having been lost in the Revolution. Lady Louisa Conolly was brought in to mediate with the old Comte de Jarnac. She agreed that £1800 a year was too small an income and that the marriage would thus not be prudent; but since the match was suitable in every other way she felt the comte should reconsider. After two months he came round, the agreement of Louis XVIII was forthcoming from his court in exile at Hartwell and the pair were married in June 1809 a the Grosvenor Place home of Isabella's grandmother, the old Duchess of Leinster.

While her husband was serving abroad with the English army, Isabella began to mix with the French court in exile, and in her journal she describes in detail a visit to Hartwell, several weeks after her marriage, to meet the future Louis XVIII. The attachments started here and the Jarnacs' high French connections benefited Isabella and her husband greatly when the Bourbons were restored to the throne of France in 1814. Louis became an aide-de-camp to the Duc d'Orléans and Isabella was eventually appointed lady-in-waiting to his duchess, who was later to become queen when the duke was enthroned as Louis Philippe.

On her husband's return from abroad she found herself living in barracks but not regretting the absence of the bare essentials her father-in-law had considered necessary for a married couple of their social standing. In 1811 the Comte and Comtesse de Rohan Chabot and their baby son set sail with the army for Lisbon and the Peninsular War. They were billeted in the curious household of the Marquis d'Anjega at Belem where the mistress of the house, the marquis's sister, Donna Marianna, had no legs and where, much to Isabella's surprise, the servants and their families were considered part of the society of the house, children ran around during dinner and beggars slept wherever they found convenient. Before Louis was ordered up-country, the marquis's chaplain, an Irishman Fr Miles Prendergast, introduced her to the nuns at the local Irish convent, all of whom, she wrote, spoke with a 'most glorious brogue'.

After four months in Portugal, Isabella and her husband, who was ill, sailed for England but were caught in a terrible storm in the Bay of Biscay and, despite having a sick baby, many leaks, blocked pumps and a hole in the side of the ship, declined to put in to France where they would be taken prisoners of war. Their child died before reaching England. They spent 1812 in Ireland visiting friends and relatives but, she wrote, as a result of the Act of Union of 1800 they found her old home, Leinster House, sadly neglected.

> We disembarked at Dunleary and reached Dublin about eleven o'clock at night in one of the national carriages called a jingle. We knocked loud and long before we obtained admittance and when we did it was with sad and solemn steps that we traversed the grass-grown court which leads from the great gate to the house. Although in the midst of a populous city we might have here quoted 'the long grass whistling in the wind', for since the union with England our family residence in town had been quite neglected and was now more like a convent than a nobleman's 'hôtel'.

Returning to England, the vicomte was pronounced unfit for active service due to ill health and they came back to Ireland in June 1813 for the birth of their daugher, Olivia, dividing their time between Carton and Leinster House.

Although her husband's estate and houses, including the Château de Jarnac, known as the Versailles du Sud, in

Charente, had been destroyed during the years of the Revolution, the couple moved to Paris after the Bourbon Restoration in 1814. They expected great things and were rather disappointed at their appointments to the House of Orléans, where the author acted as dame for five years.

Isabella nevertheless gave long descriptions in her journal of the people she met there, who included the royal family, the Duke of Wellington and his wife, Kitty Pakenham, a friend from Dublin days, and of the current fashions.

In a letter she describes how her mother-in-law made her 'presentable' to Paris society:

> You must know that nobody is considered so at Paris until completely Frenchised in dress, so that I must submit to wearing a bonnet as high as the Sugar Loaf hill, near Dublin, and having my waist up to my chin! As yet I have been seen only by a few very intimate friends of Mme de Jarnac's who are as much interested in the reform of my dress as if the restoration of our property depended on it. In short, it is by these narrow-minded people considered quite ridiculous to be dressed à l'Anglaise. 'Eh bien, je ne la trouve pas si ridicule' was the expression which I heard Mme La Comtesse de Noailles make use of in a half whisper as I turned about to reach a chair.

Isabella moved in the highest levels of society with her Irish mother-in-law, the Comtesse de Jarnac, who had endured the years of Revolution and of Napoleon in France in a fruitless attempt to save the Jarnac estates. At one stage this former Elizabeth Smyth of Wicklow shared a cell at Carmes with the future Empress Josephine.

Isabella's journal is full of the gossip of the day, often in the form of letters. A princess dies when her petticoats catch fire and, to Isabella's surprise, everyone rushed to the house to give their condolences:

> To us these visits would appear an intrusion but it suits the French to give way to their grief in this manner. I have often observed in France that the first impulse is to go to people in affliction and if not sufficiently nearly related that 'le premier besoin est de se

faire écrire'. With them it is a sort of sacred duty – like a mass for the soul!

The bodies of the king's brother and sister-in-law, Louis XVI and Marie Antoinette, were dug up and removed to the royal tomb at St Denis, she writes. It was January and freezing yet all the troops had to stand for hours, and the cathedral itself was deadly cold.

> Maréchal Ney was heard to say that he never experienced half as much inconvenience during the whole Russian campaign as he did from the cold of St Denis yesterday in full dress. In Russia at least he was muffled up in furs. (P.S. One gentleman really died of cold soon after he got home.)

When news arrived of Napoleon's escape from Elba and march northward, Paris was in turmoil and the royalists fled. The calmness of the Duchess of Wellington, who was deemed to be in great danger, "formed a striking contrast with the violent agitation of most of the French ladies that I have met with, who each exclaimed with Madame la Princess de Talleyrand, 'Moi, je serai la première victime.'"

Isabella was soon to be confined again and, as her husband was abroad with the army of the Duc d'Orléans, she decided to quit Paris. "I really feel for those I leave behind though the long faces and dishevelled hair of some of the generally well-powdered royalists is, it must be confessed, amusing and ridiculous."

A few hours before Napoleon entered Paris on 20 March 1815, Isabella, her baby daughter and two maids, one French, one Irish, fled a city where the citizens were removing *fleur-de-lis* and replacing them with Napoleonic arms. After a nightmarish journey, seeking fresh horses and presenting her passport at each town, they embarked for Dover at Calais. Meeting with Louis in London, they took a 72-hour boat journey from Liverpool to Dublin and at Carton two weeks later Isabella gave birth to her son Philippe (later to be the French ambassador to London).

After Waterloo, Isabella and her husband returned to Paris and as she was officially appointed a lady-in-waiting to the Duchesse d'Orléans – a position which did not greatly please her – they took up residence at the Palais Royal and at the Château de Villiers in Neuilly. A second daughter was born in 1820. She describes the life at court as monotonous compared with the agitation of the public mind at the continued occupation of Wellington's army. After four years in Paris the family took an extended trip home and she later described the 1821 visit to Ireland of George IV and her passage back to England with him in the royal yacht.

> There never was such a scene of heartfelt joy as poor deserted Dublin presented during the king's visit. He was accompanied by many of the corps diplomatique and many a native face was seen in the streets of Dublin which had seldom been witnessed there since the throw [the 1800 Act of Union].
>
> Everything said and done on this occasion appeared natural and as if it came from the heart. There was nothing theatrical or for stage effect. How unlike 'l'entrée du roi' at Paris. The king gave away two or three ribands of the order of St Patrick but one never heard of his being persecuted with applications of any nature during his visit to Ireland. The pleasure of seeing him there seemed sufficient in itself.

Isabella ended her journal on a melancholy note:

> From the lips of him to whom I devoted fourteen years of my life and whom I followed in perils by sea and perils by land, have I heard the sentence that 'whatever he chooses to do, it is no longer any personal concern of mine'. So be it – released from all responsibility on earth my mind soars above this world and seeks for rest where alone true joys are to be found.

It was 1825, she was forty-two years old. Life was on the ebb:

> I feel thankful that so much of my race is run and that I am becoming a respectable middle-aged woman having passed through camps and courts (by grace of God) with unblemished reputation. Lonely and cheerless was my life when I first took up my pen, nineteen years ago at Cheltenham in 1806. Lonely and cheerless would

my exile now be were it not for my promising and affectionate children.

Her journal may have ended but her life certainly did not. The throne of France passed to the Orléans branch of the Bourbons and she became chief lady-in-waiting to Queen Marie Amélie, wife of Louis Philippe, the Duc d'Orléans to whom she and Louis had given so much service.

Isabella's daughter Olivia married Jules de Lasteyrie, grandson of Lafayette, and came to live at the Château de Lagrange. When her brother Philippe, who had no descendants, died in 1875 having inherited Thomastown Castle in Co. Tipperary from his paternal cousin, Lady Elizabeth Mathew, one of the Smyth sisters, Olivia gave up her interest in the castle in exchange for receiving all her brother's papers from his widow.

The papers were removed to Lagrange where the Comte de Chambrun and his wife, Josée, daughter of Pierre Laval (Prime Minister of France during the 1930s and chief minister of the Vichy government), later discovered them and sorted them with the help of the Vicomte Olivier de Rohan Chabot, a descendant of the Duc de Rohan, the old Comte de Jarnac's elder brother. The Comte de Chambrun had inherited Lagrange from his uncle, Louis de Lasteyrie, Olivia's grandson. Among the papers was Isabella's journal.

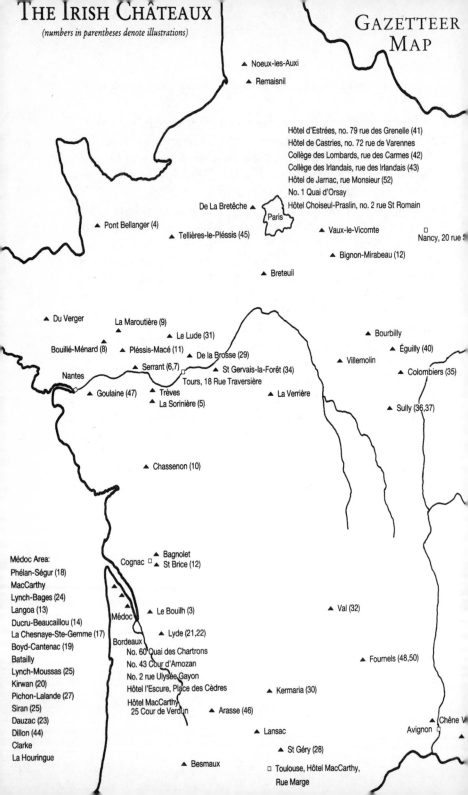

THE IRISH CHÂTEAUX

(numbers in parentheses denote illustrations)

GAZETTEER
MAP

Noeux-les-Auxi

Remaisnil

Hôtel d'Estrées, no. 79 rue des Grenelle (41)
Hôtel de Castries, no. 72 rue de Varennes
Collège des Lombards, rue des Carmes (42)
Collège des Irlandais, rue des Irlandais (43)
Hôtel de Jarnac, rue Monsieur (52)
No. 1 Quai d'Orsay
Hôtel Choiseul-Praslin, no. 2 rue St Romain

De La Bretêche

Paris

Pont Bellanger (4)

Tellières-le-Pléssis (45)

Vaux-le-Vicomte

Nancy, 20 rue

Bignon-Mirabeau (12)

Breteuil

Du Verger

La Maroutière (9)

Le Lude (31)

Bourbilly

Bouillé-Ménard (8)

Pléssis-Macé (11)

De la Brosse (29)

Éguilly (40)

Villemolin

Nantes

Serrant (6,7)

St Gervais-la-Forêt (34)

Tours, 18 Rue Traversière

Colombiers (35)

Goulaine (47)

Trèves

La Sorinière (5)

La Verrière

Sully (36,37)

Chassenon (10)

Bagnolet

Cognac

St Brice (12)

Médoc Area:
Phélan-Ségur (18)
MacCarthy
Lynch-Bages (24)
Langoa (13)
Ducru-Beaucaillou (14)
La Chesnaye-Ste-Gemme (17)
Boyd-Cantenac (19)
Batailly
Lynch-Moussas (25)
Kirwan (20)
Pichon-Lalande (27)
Siran (25)
Dauzac (23)
Dillon (44)
Clarke
La Houringue

Médoc

Le Bouilh (3)

Lyde (21,22)

Val (32)

Bordeaux
No. 60 Quai des Chartrons
No. 43 Cour d'Arnozan
No. 2 Ulysée Gayon
Hôtel l'Escure, Place des Cèdres
Hôtel MacCarthy
25 Cour de Verdun

Fournels (48,50)

Kermaria (30)

Arasse (46)

Chêne V

Lansac

Avignon

St Géry (28)

Besmaux

Toulouse, Hôtel MacCarthy,
Rue Marge

GAZETTEER

ARASSE (Chapter Twelve) Foulayronnes, 47000 Agen, Lot-et-Garonne. Baron Dillon Kavanagh de Feartagh. Private.

BAGNOLET (Chapter Four) Cognac, Charente. Property of Jas. Hennessy and Co. Private. Reserved for clients.

BESMAUX (Chapter Twelve) near Auch, Gers. A château of the Dillons of Terrefour. Private.

BIGNON-MIRABEAU (Chapter One) 452210 Ferrières-en-Gatinais, Seine et Marne. 25 kilometres east of Nemours. La Comtesse de la Tour du Pin. Open 2.30 pm – 6.30 pm, Saturday to Monday, from 1 July to 1 October.

BORDEAUX (Chapters Five and Six)
    no. 60 Quai des Chartrons. Offices of Daniel and Hugues Lawton.
    no. 43 Cour d'Arnozan. Built Abraham Lawton c. 1750. Private.
    no. 2 rue Ulysée Gayon. Eighteenth-century town house of Jean Jacques Lynch. Private.
    Hôtel L'Escure, Place des Cèdres, nineteenth-century villa of the Johnston family. Now a hospital.
    Hôtel MacCarthy, 25 Cour de Verdun. Private.

BOUILH, LE (Chapter One) N 4064 St André-de-Cubzac, Gironde. M. Feuilhade de Chauvin. 25 kilometres east of Bordeaux. Open Thurs., Sat. and Sun. from May to September 2.30 pm – 6.30 pm. Tel: 57 43 0659

BOUILLÉ-MÉNARD (Chapter Three) 10 kilometres Segré, Pays de Loire. Duc de Walsh Serrant. Open on request. Tel: 41 61 6273.

BOURBILLY (Chapter Eight) Epoisses 21460, Côte d'Or. Owner Mme d'Arcy. Open 10 am – 12 pm and 3 pm – 6 pm.

BOYD-CANTENAC (Chapter Five) Pouget Margaux, Médoc. Pierre Guillemet. Tel: 56 88 3058 (wine).

BRETEUIL (Chapter Thirteen) Choiseul-Chevreuse 78460, Isle de France. Marquis de Breteuil. Open daily. Tel: 052 0511.

BRETÊCHE, DE LA (Chapter Fourteen) Nom-de-la-Bretêche, Seine et Oise. Baron Guillaume. Private.

BROSSE, DE LA (Chapter Seven) 37380 Monnaie, Indre-et-Loire. Mlles MacCarthy. Private.

CHASSENON (Chapter Three) near Niort, Deux Sèvres. M. Masson. Private.

CHÊNE VERT (Chapter Nine) Villeneuve-les-Avignon, Languedoc-Roussillon. M. Simonnet. Private.

CHESNAYE-STE-GEMME (Chapter Five) 33460 Margaux, Médoc. On the grounds of the Château Lanessan, which is owned by M. Hubert Bouteiller. Tel:56 58 9480

CLARKE (Chapter Five) Listrac 33480, Castelnau de Médoc. Baron Edmund de Rothschild. Tel: 56 88 8800

COLOMBIERS (Chapter Nine) Bligny-sur-Ouche, Côte d'Or. Comte de Wall. Private.

DAUZAC (Chapter Six) Labarde 33460 Margaux, Médoc. M. F. Chatellier. Tel: 56 88 3210. Open daily 9 am – 12 pm and 2 pm – 5 pm (wine).

DILLON or LE TERREFOUR (Chapter Twelve) Blanquefort, Bordeaux. Lycée Agricole. Tel: 56 35 0227. Open on arrangement (wine).

DUCRU BEAUCAILLOU (Chapter Five) St Julien, Médoc. M. Borie. Tel: 56 59 0520 for visits (wine).

ÉGUILLY (Chapter Ten) On the A 6 autoroute east of Dijon near turn to Semur-en-Auxois. M. Roger Aubry. Art gallery open to public.

FONTAINE (Chapter Nine) Senlis 60300, Oise. Comte Marc de Warren. Private.

FOURNELS (Chapter Thirteen) 48310 Fournels, Lozère. Marquis de Brion. Private.

GOULAINE (Chapter Thirteen) Haute Goulaine 44115, 18 kilometres south-east of Nantes. Marquis de Goulaine. Open daily from 18 June to 16 September, 2 pm – 6.30 pm. Open weekends from 21 April to 4 November (also wine). Tel: 40 54 9142

HOURINGUE, LA (Chapter Five) Macau, Médoc. Mme Touchand. Private.

KERMARIA (Chapter Eight) Villefranche, Aveyron. Comte de Butler. Private.

KIRWAN (Chapter Five) Margaux, Médoc. Société Schröder et Schÿler. Tel: 56 81 2410 for visits (wine).

LANGOA (Chapter Five) St Julien, Médoc. Anthony Barton. Visit by appointment. Tel: 56 59 0605 (wine).

LANSAC (Chapter Two) Merles, Tarn et Garonne. Formerly O'Kelly-Farrell family. Private.

LUDE, LE (Chapter Eight) 72800 Le Lude, Sarthe. Marquis de Nicolay. Open 3 pm – 6 pm from 1 April to 30 September.

LYDE (Chapter Six) Cadillac, Gironde. M. et Mme Garaud. Private.

LYNCH-BAGES (Chapter Six) Pauillac, Médoc. M. Cazes. Tel: 56 59 1919. Open 9 am – 12 pm and 2 pm – 5 pm (wine).

LYNCH-MOUSSAS (Chapter Six) Pauillac, Médoc. M. Casteja. Tel: 56 59 5714. Open 8 am – 12 pm and 2 pm – 6 pm (wine).

MACCARTHY (Chapter Five) St Estèphe, Médoc. Open by appointment (wine).

MAROUTIÈRE, LA (Chapter Three) Château Gauntier, Mayenne. Comte and Comtesse Walsh de Serrant. Private.

MARY (Chapter Eleven) Aix-en-Provence, Provence. Formerly St Leger family. Private.

NANCY (Chapter Nine) no. 20 rue St Michel, Nancy, Lorraine. Formerly town-house of the Warrens. Private.

NOEUX LES AUXI (Chapter Eight) Pas de Calais. Comte Tanguy de Butler. Private.

The Irish Châteaux

NEUILLY (Chapter Fourteen) no. 52 Boulevard d'Argenson at the junction with Boulevard de Saussaye. Site of the Orléans château demolished 1848.

PARIS

Hôtel d'Estrées (Chapter One) no. 79 rue de Grenelle, Septième. Residence of the Duc de Feltre. Now Russian Embassy.

Hôtel de Castries (Chapter Ten) no. 72 rue de Varennes, Septième. Birthplace of Marshal MacMahon, Duc de Magenta. Now Ministry of Defence.

Collège des Lombards (Chapter Eleven) rue des Carmes, Cinquième. Now Syrian church of St Epreux.

Collège des Irlandais (Chapter Eleven) rue des Irlandais, Cinquième. Fr Swords. By appointment. Tel: 43 31 3265.

Hôtel de Jarnac (Chapter Fourteen) rue Monsieur, Septième. Private.

no. 1 Quai d'Orsay (Chapter One) Septième. Residence of the Abbé Edgeworth, Longford-born confessor to Louis XVI. Private.

Hôtel de Choiseul-Praslin (Chapter Thirteen) no. 2 rue St Romain, Cinquième. Now Post Office headquarters. Tel. M. Ferièrres at 45 64 0431

PHÉLAN-SÉGUR (Chapter Five) St Estèphe, Médoc. Former château of Phelans.

PICHON-LALANDE (Chapter Six) Pauillac, Médoc. Mme de Lencquesaing. Open by appointment for wine. Tel: 56 59 1940

PLÉSSIS-MACÉ (Chapter Three) 13 kilometres north of Angers, Maine et Loire. Property of the Départment. Open 1 March to 30 November from 2 pm – 6 pm. and from 1 July to 30 September also 10 am – 12 pm. Tel: 41 91 6408.

PONT BELLANGER (Chapter One) St Sever, Calvados. Comte O'Mahony. Private.

REMAISNIL (Chapter Eight) Remaisnil Picardie. Formerly Butler. Private.

Gazetteer

ST BRICE (Chapter Four) 16100 Cognac, Charente. Kilian Hennessy. Gardens open for *son et lumière* in June.

ST GERVAIS-LA-FORÊT (Chapter Nine) Blois, Loir-et-Cher. Comte de Warren. Private.

ST-GÉRY (Chapter Seven) 81800 Rabestens, Tarn. M. and Mme O'Byrne. Open 1 April to 1 November Sunday afternoons and open every day in July and August. Tel: 63 33 7043.

SEGONZAC (Chapter Two) Riberac, Dordogne. Baron de Segonzac. Private.

SERRANT (Chapter Three) St Georges de Loire, Maine-et-Loire. Prince de Ligne. Open from 20 March to 31 October 9 am – 11.30 am and 2 pm – 6 pm. Tel: 41 39 1301.

SIRAN (Chapter Six) Margaux, Médoc. M. Miailhe. Open 9 am – 11.30 am and 2.30 – 5.30 (wine). Tel: 56 81 3501.

SORINIÈRE, LA (Chapter Two) Chemillé, Maine-et-Loire. M. and Mme O'Kelly-Farrell. Chapel open to public.

SULLY (Chapter Ten) 71360 Épinac, Côte d'Or. Duc de Magenta. Exterior only open.

TELLIÈRES-LE-PLÉSSIS (Chapter Twelve) Orne. M. Dillon-Corneck. Private.

TOULOUSE (Chapter Seven) Hôtel MacCarthy, rue Marge. M. de Vicoise. Private.

TOURS (Chapter Two) no. 18 rue Traversie. M. Browne de Kilmaine. Private.

TRÈVES (Chapter Two) St Cunault, Maine-et-Loire. National Monument. Open to public.

VAL (Chapter Eight) Lanobre 15270, Bort-les-Orgues, Cantal. Property of the Départment. Open 15 June to 15 September from 9 am – 12 pm and 2 pm – 6.30 pm.

VAUX LE VICOMTE (Chapter Thirteen) Melun, Seine et Marne. Marquis de Vogue. Open 1 April to 30 October from 10 am – 6 pm. Fountains second and fourth Saturday each month. Tel: 60 66 9709.

VERGER, LE (Chapter Three) Blain, Ille et Vilaine. Comte Alberic de Walsh Serrant. Private.

VERRIÉRE, LA (Chapter Fourteen) Oizon 18700, Cher. Home for several years of Emily, Duchess of Leinster, and her children including Lord Edward Fitzgerald. Now owned by M. de Vogue. Open from 15 February to 15 November from 10 am – 12 pm and from 2 pm – 7 pm. Tel: 48 58 0691.

VILLEMOLIN (Chapter Twelve) Anthien 58800, Nièvre. Marquis de Certaines. Open 1 May to 1 November from 10 am – 12 pm and 2 pm – 6 pm.

A SUPPLEMENTARY LISTING, 1999

ARCELOT Arceau, Cote d'Or. Neo-Classical château set in an 1830 English park designed for Philibert Verchere in 1761 by Thomas Domorey. Inherited by the Loisy family who are descended from the Cleres whose Irish inheritance has come down to the Rosse family in Birr. Open to public. Forman's film *Liaisons Dangereuses* would have been shot there had not the present Comte de Loisy re-read the novel the night before.

HERNICOURT near Arras, Artois. Built in 1846 for the Roussel family. Acquired in 1885 by Pauline Tierny, their cousin, who disrupted its sobriety with an incongruous wing, possibly by her son Emile, who certainly designed its neo-Gothic model farm. Badly damaged in both world wars.

LESSAY-LES-CHÂTEAU Mayenne. Moated medieval fortress constructed in 1458 for Jehan de Vendome. Remodelled as a chateâu. Inherited by a branch of the FitzGeralds.

LE FAYAL near Compiegne, Picardy. Château built in 1650 for Philippe de La Mothe Houdancourt by Jacques Bruant and completed in 1656, when Louis XIV received Queen Christina of Sweden. Inherited in 1819 by the future Marquise de Walsh Serrant whose grand-daughter, the last Duchesse de La Mothe Houdancourt (1861-1940), married a cousin Valentine Hussey Walsh. Restored by her grand-nephew. Open on request.

ROUSSET Clomot, Cote d'Or. Built c.1400 for Jean Rousset and remodelled c.1650 for Louis de Villers-La Faye. Inherited by McCarthies who died out c.1940. Now being carefully restored by M. and Mme Michel Guyon.

FURTHER READING

Bence Jones, Mark, *Twilight of the Ascendancy* (London 1987, pbk 1993).

Bonaparte Wyse, Olga, *The Spurious Brood* (London 1969).

Cullen, L.M, 'The Irish Merchant Communities at Bordeaux, La Rochelle and Cognac in the Eighteenth Century' in Cullen and P. Butel (eds) *Négoce et Industrie en France et en Irelande aux XVII et XIX siècles* (Paris 1980).

—, 'The Dublin Merchant Community' in Cullen and P. Butel (eds), *Cities and Merchants: French and Irish Perspectives on Urban Development 1500-1800* (Dublin 1986).

—, *Irish Diaspora in the 17th-18th centuries: Europeans on the Move 1500-1800,* ed. Nicholas Canny (Oxford 1995).

—, *The Brandy Trade under the Ancien Régime: Regional Specialisation in the Charente* (Cambridge 1998)

—, *The Irish Brandy Houses of Eighteenth-Century France* (The Lilliput Press, Dublin, forthcoming 2000)

Dickson, David and Gough, Hugh, *The French Revolution and the Irish Brigades* (Irish Academic Press, Dublin 1990).

Elliott, Marianne, *Partners in Revolution – The United Irishmen and France* (New Haven and London 1982).

—, *Wolfe Tone, Prophet of Irish Independence* (London 1989).

Hachette Châteaux de France, series of eight volumes.

Harcourt, Felice (ed.), *Memoirs of Madame de la Tour du Pin* (London 1989).

Harris, R.G, 'The Irish Regiments, A Pictorial History (1683-1987)', *Irish Sword* XVIII (72).

Hayes, Richard, *Ireland and Irishmen in the French Revolution* (Dublin 1932).

—, *Old Irish Links with France* (Dublin 1940).

—, *Biographical Dictionary of Irishmen in France* (Dublin 1949).

Hennessy, Maurice N., *The Wild Geese, The Irish Soldier in Exile* (London 1973).

Kee, Robert, *The Most Distressful Country* (London 1976).

Kerney Walsh, Micheline, *Destruction by Peace* (R.&S. Printers, Monaghan 1986).

—, 'Letters from Fontenoy', *Irish Sword* (78) 1995.

McDermot, Frank, 'Arthur O'Connor' in *Irish Historical Studies*, vol. xv, no. 77 (Dublin 1966).

McDonnell, Hector, *The Wild Geese of the Antrim MacDonnells* (Irish Academic Press, Dublin 1999).

McLaughlin, Mark G., *The Wild Geese – The Irish Brigades of France and Spain* (London 1980).

—, and Warner, Chris, 'The Wild Geese, The Irish Brigades of France and Spain', *Irish Sword* XVI (62).

Miailhe, W.A.B., editor of the pamphlets '*Les Irlandais en Aquitaine*' and '*Le Comte J.B. Lynch, Maire de Bordeaux 1809-1815*' (Bordeaux 1970 and 1971).

O'hAnnrachain, Eoghan, 'The FitzJames Cavalry Regiment', *Irish Sword* (78) 1995.

O'Callaghan, Cornelius, *History of the Irish Brigades in the Service of France* (Glasgow 1870, reprinted I.U.P., Shannon 1969).

O'Connor, Arthur, *The State of Ireland*, ed. James Livesey (The Lilliput Press, Dublin 1998).

Seely, James, *Great Bordeaux Wines* (London 1986).

Simms, J.G., 'The Irish on the Continent, 1691-1800' in Moody and Vaughan (eds), *A New History of Ireland*, iv (Oxford 1986).

Swords, Liam, *The Green Cockade: The Irish in the French Revolution* (Dublin 1989).

Tierny Gilbert, *La Famille Tierney de l'Irlande a l'Artois 1690-1990* (Imprimérie de Moulin 1991).

Tillyard, Stella, *Citizen Lord Edward FitzGerald 1763-1798* (Chatto and Windus 1997).

Life of Theobald Wolfe Tone: Memoirs, Journals and Political Writings, compiled and arranged by William T.W. Tone, 1826, ed. Thomas Bartlett (The Lilliput Press, Dublin 1998).